MW01702649

Horizons

Preschool

For Three's

Student Workbook

Author/Editor: Rachelle Wiersma, M.A.

Managing Editor: Alan Christopherson, M.S.

Copy Editors: Pamela Ufen
Anita Lanning

Designer & Illustrator: Anthony Kuhlmann

Alpha Omega Publications • Rock Rapids, Iowa

804 N. 2nd Ave. E., Rock Rapids, IA 51246-1759

Printed in the United States of America

ISBN 978-0-7403-2996-8

PREFACE

The Horizons Preschool For Three's Student Workbook contains activities to help the student in skill development. Each Horizons Preschool For Three's lesson includes four worksheets in this book along with one worksheet on heavier stock that is in the ***Student Workbook Companion.*** Some of the worksheets in the ***Student Workbook Companion*** have an activity that is designed to be repeated by the student throughout the lesson as well as beyond. Each lesson also includes a worksheet that supplements the Bible lesson.

The abilities of a three-year-old student will vary greatly. Some will be able to write, trace, and color. Others will not or as they move forward in the course their motor skills will develop. The expectations for what a student is able to do on each of the worksheets should fit their abilities. Some of the matching activities might have to be completed orally or dotted lines can be drawn on the page for the student to trace. Some students will be able to use a pencil but for most a crayon might be best.

The handwriting activities might be too much to ask of a student of this age. There is plenty of time to develop penmanship in later years so don't feel that this has to be mastered. Tracing letters with a finger is fine and it is also OK if you hold their hand and guide it through the letter formation.

The most important thing is to make the learning experience fun and enjoyable.

Contents

Contents

LESSON 1

WORKSHEETS 1-4

Bible Story: Creation, Genesis 1-2

LESSON 1

WORKSHEET 1

NAME McKenna

Trace the word cat with your finger. Color the cat.

cat

NAME

LESSON 1
WORKSHEET 2

Match the animals that are the same.
The student can do this either verbally or by drawing a line.

Count each group of cats. Circle the picture of one cat.
Color the cats.

Draw a picture of yourself.
Have an adult help write your name.

NAME

NAME

LESSON 1
WORKSHEET 4

Have the student color the birds, lion, and fish on the scene of creation below.

LESSON 2

WORKSHEETS 6–9

Bible Story: Sin, Genesis 3

NAME

Trace the word dog with your finger. Color the dog.

dog

NAME

Circle the largest dog on the sheet. Color the dogs.

Count each group of dogs. Circle the group of two dogs.
Color the dogs.

NAME

Match the colors that are the same.
The student can do this either verbally or by drawing a line.

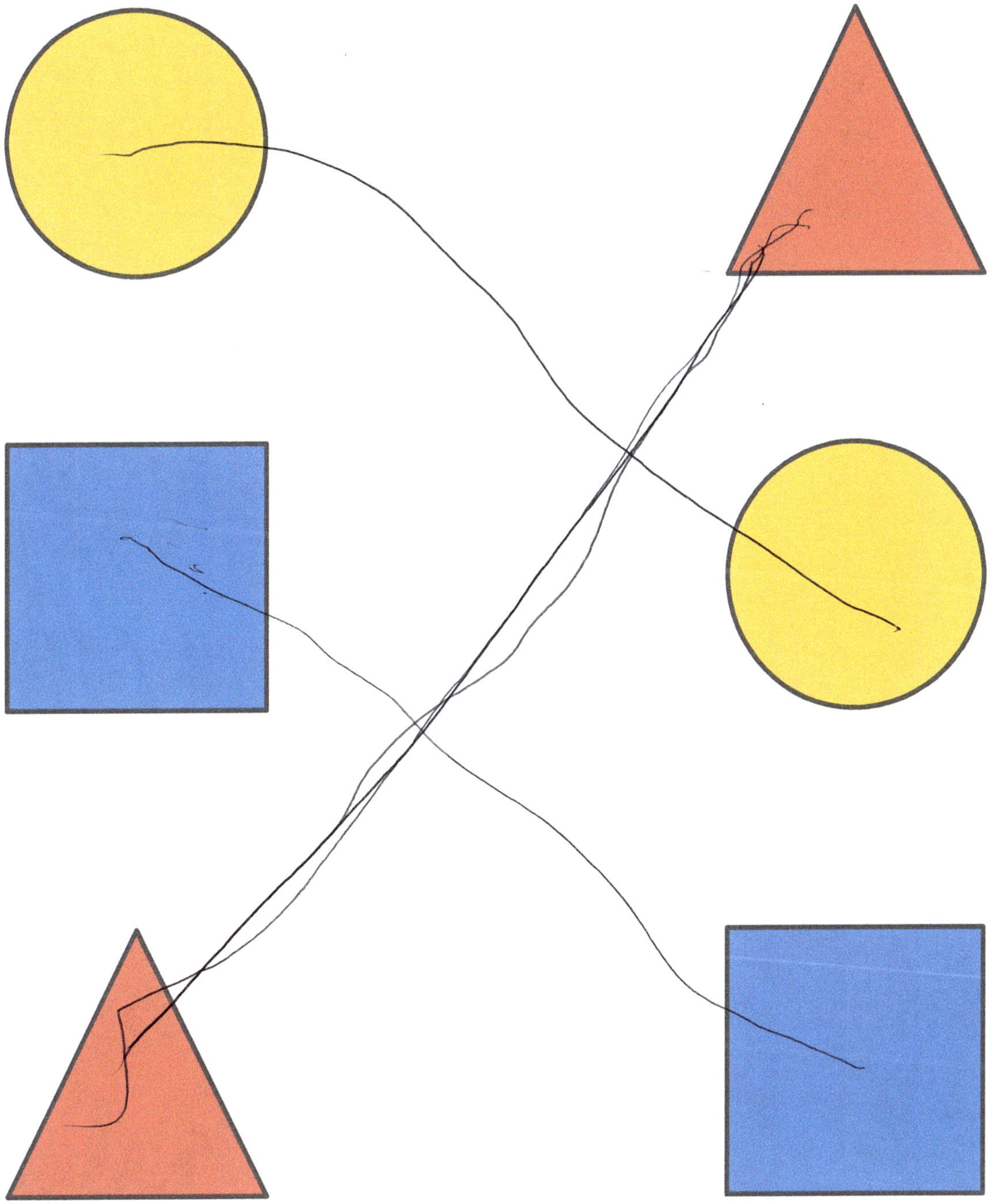

Put a black mark over the weeds. Circle the flowers.

NAME

After Adam and Eve sinned, Nature was no longer perfect. Draw some weeds in the picture. Make some of the water and sky dirty.

LESSON 3

WORKSHEETS 11–14

Bible Story: Noah, Genesis 6:1–9:17

NAME

Trace the word pig with your finger. Color the pig.

pig

NAME

LESSON 3
WORKSHEET 12

Match the pigs that are the same.
The student can do this either verbally or by drawing a line.

Count the pigs in each group. Circle the group of three pigs.
Color the pigs.

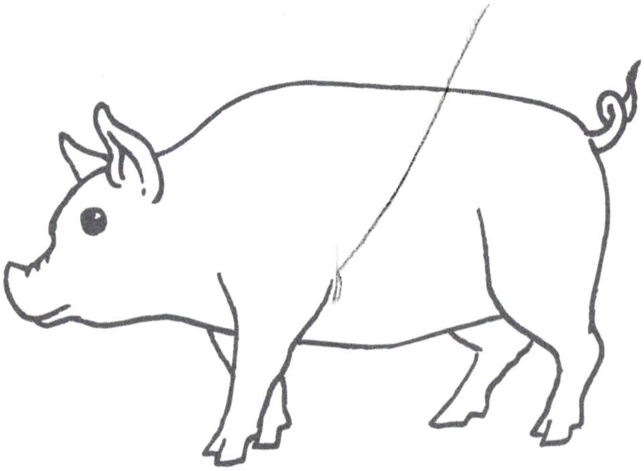

NAME

Match the shapes. After you are finished,
Color the same shapes with the same color.

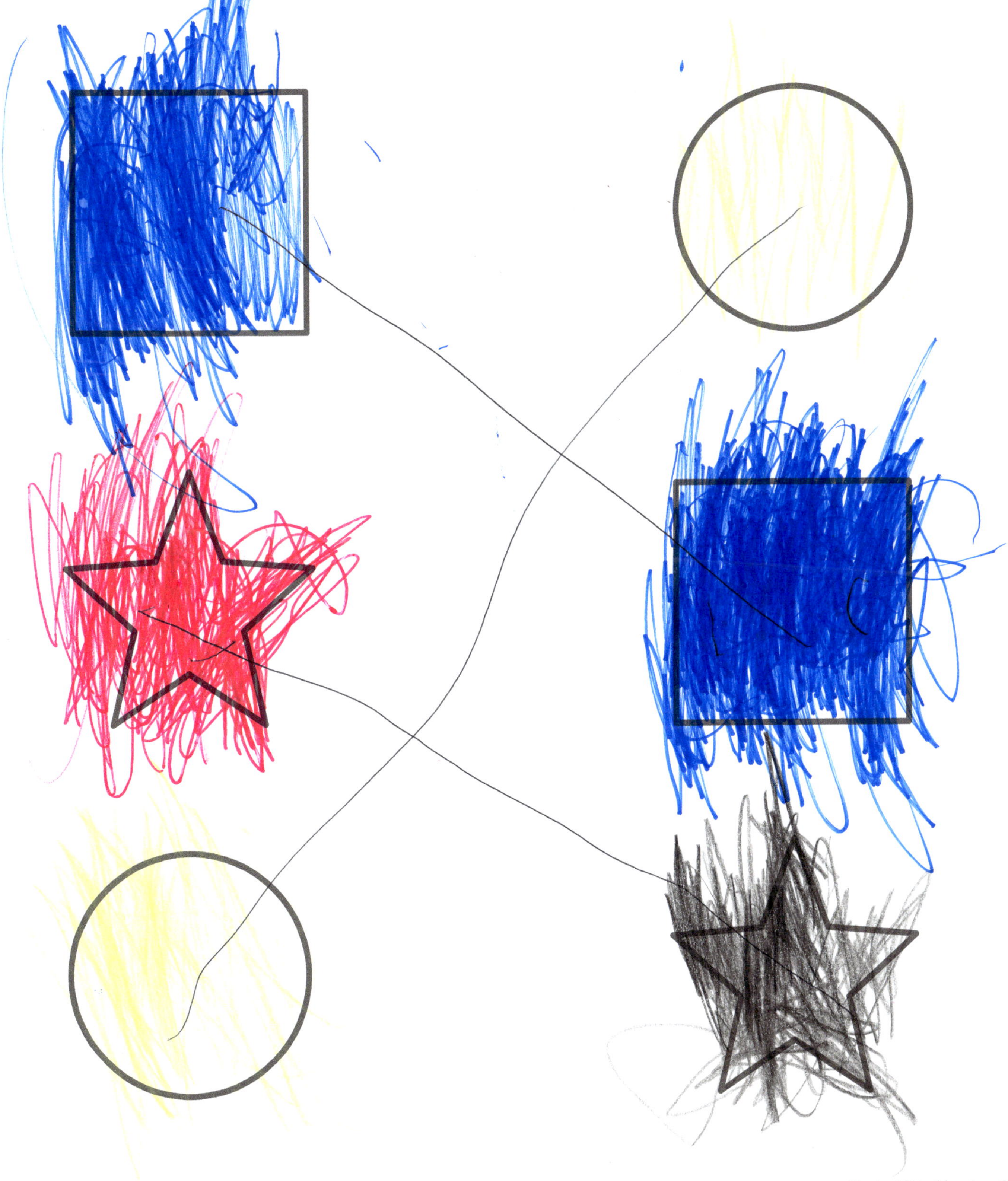

Circle the largest item in each row.
Put an X on the smallest item in each row.

NAME

Color the animals going into the ark.

LESSON 4

WORKSHEETS 16-19

Bible Story: Tower of Babel, Genesis 11:1-9

NAME

Trace the word duck with your finger. Color the duck yellow.

duck

NAME

Circle the yellow duck.

Circle the green duck.

Circle the blue duck.

Trace the number 1. Trace the word one with your finger.
Count the number of ducks. Color the number 1.

1

one

NAME

LESSON 4
WORKSHEET 18

Circle the smallest tower. Color the largest tower.

Count each group of ducks. Circle the picture of one duck.
Color the ducks.

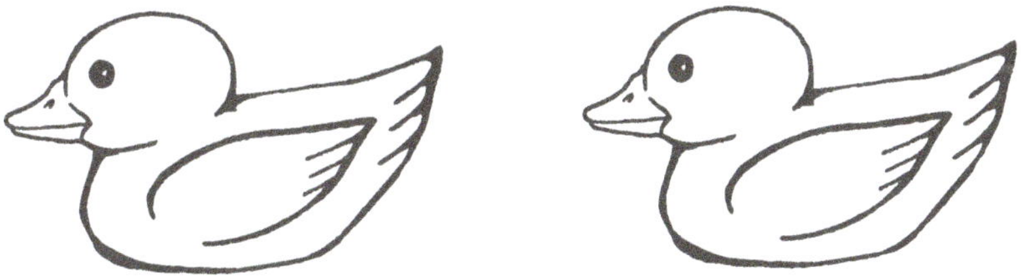

In the picture below, have the student identify the mom, dad, and baby.

NAME

Color the Tower of Babel picture.

LESSON 5

WORKSHEETS 21–24

Bible Story: Moses, Exodus 2:1–10

NAME

Trace the word cow with your finger. Color the cow.

cow

NAME

LESSON 5
WORKSHEET 22

Trace the number 2. Trace the word two with your finger.
Count the number of cows. Color the number 2.

2

two

Identify the following people in the picture:
mother, father, children, grandmother, and grandfather.

NAME

LESSON 5
WORKSHEET 23

Point to the cow that is under the cloud. Point to the cow that is next to the tree. Point to the cow that is on the grass. Color the cows.

Count each group of camels. Circle the picture of three camels.
Color the camels.

NAME

Circle the following objects in the picture:
baby, crown, pyramids, sandals, and basket.

LESSON 6

WORKSHEETS 26-29

Bible Story: Burning Bush, Exodus 2:11-4:17

LESSON 6
WORKSHEET 26

NAME

Trace the word sun with your finger. Color the sun.

sun

NAME

Trace the number 3. Trace the word three with your finger.
Count the number of suns. Color the number 3.

3

three

Identify the head, arms, legs, feet, and hands on the person.

NAME

Color the sun in the sky.
Color the flowers in the picture.

Draw a line to match the color with fruit that is the same color.
Name the colors. Name the fruits.

NAME

Color the picture of Moses and the burning bush.

LESSON 7

WORKSHEETS 31–34

Bible Story: Plagues, Exodus 5:1–13:16

LESSON 7
WORKSHEET 31

NAME

Trace the word star with your finger.
Count the points on the star. Color the star.

star

NAME

LESSON 7
WORKSHEET 32

Circle the glasses that are full of juice.
Put an X over the glasses that are empty.

Match the clothing items. The student can do this either verbally or by drawing a line.

NAME

Count and color four stars in the picture.

Draw a line between the items which have the same two colors.

NAME

Find the plagues in the picture.

LESSON 8

WORKSHEETS 36-39

Bible Story: Red Sea, Exodus 13:17-15:21

NAME

Trace the word moon with your finger. Color the moon.

moon

NAME

Color the moon in the picture yellow. Color the stars blue.

Circle the group of five moons. Color the moons.

NAME ______________________________

Circle the largest star in the top row. Circle the largest moon in the middle row. Circle the largest sun in the bottom row. When you are finished, color the pictures.

Match the items you would use for a meal.

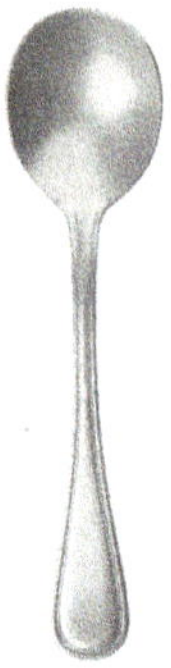

NAME

With a brown crayon, draw a dry path down the middle of the picture.

LESSON 9

WORKSHEETS 41–44

Bible Story: Food in the Desert, Exodus 16

NAME

Trace the word car with your finger. Color the car.

car

NAME

LESSON 9
WORKSHEET 42

Trace the number 4. Trace the word four with your finger.
Count the number of cars. Color the number 4.

4

four

Circle the objects which do not belong in the room.

NAME

Count the number of tires on the car.
Color the tires black.
Count the number of windows on the car.
Color the windows yellow.
Count the number of stars on the car.
Color the stars green.

Color or circle the picture that is different in each row.

NAME

Use a brown crayon to draw over the dashed lines to form the baskets. Color the rest of the picture.

LESSON 10

WORKSHEETS 46-49

Bible Story: A New Home, Joshua 1-4

LESSON 10
WORKSHEET 46

NAME

Trace the word train with your finger. Color the train.

train

NAME

Trace the number 5. Trace the word five with your finger.
Count the number of engines. Color the number 5.

5

five

Match the socks that belong together.

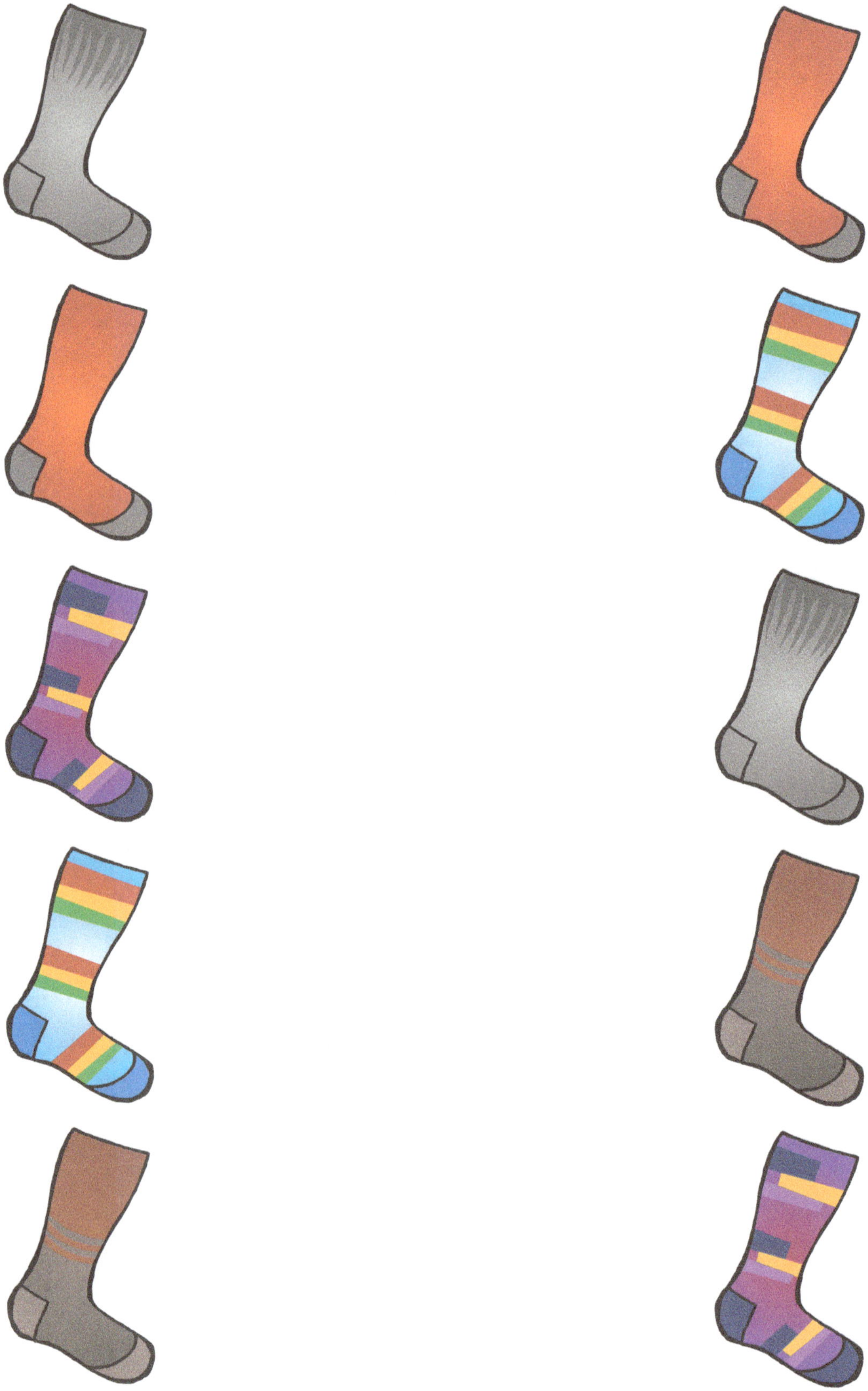

NAME

Count the number of train cars.
Color the train when you are finished.

Name each food on the sheet.
Match the foods that are the same kind.
The student can do this either verbally or by drawing a line.

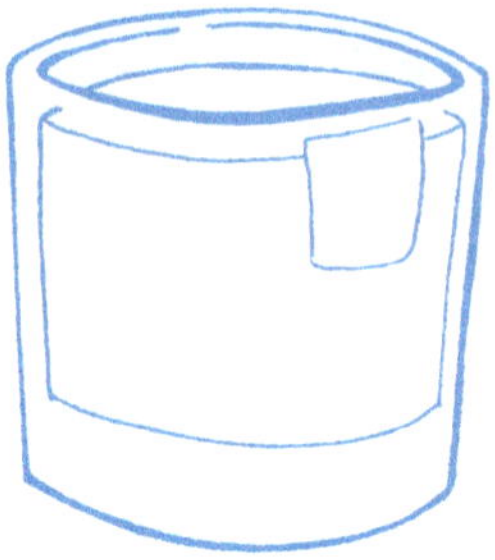

NAME

Follow the maze taking God's people to the Promised Land.

LESSON 11

WORKSHEETS 51-54

Bible Story: Jericho, Joshua 6

LESSON 11
WORKSHEET 51

NAME

Trace the word truck with your finger. Color the truck.

truck

NAME

LESSON 11
WORKSHEET 52

Match the number to the number of items.
The student can do this either verbally or by drawing a line.

1

2

3

4

5

Circle the group of six trucks. Color the trucks.

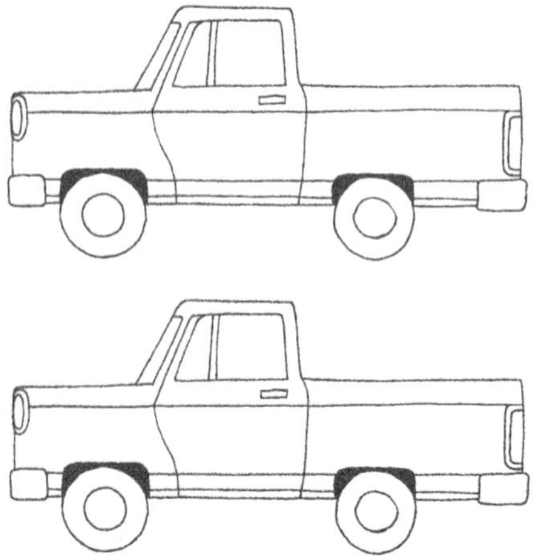

NAME

If the food is the correct color, say yes. If it is wrong, say no.

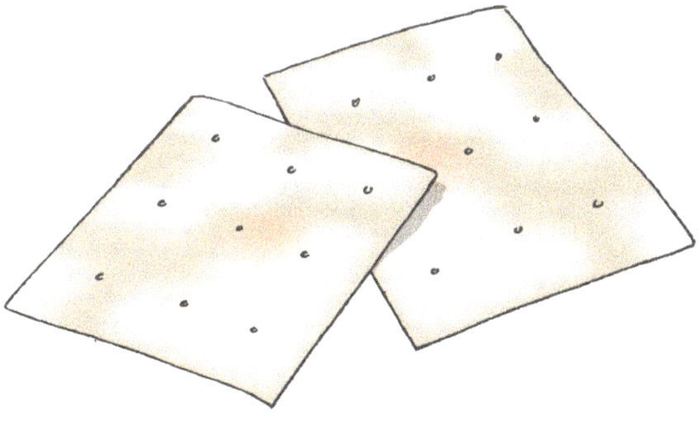

Identify what's missing in the following pictures.

NAME

Find a wheel, trumpet, rope, dog, and coin in the picture.
Color the picture.

LESSON 12

WORKSHEETS 56-59

Bible Story: Hannah's Prayer, 1 Samuel 1

LESSON 12
WORKSHEET 56

NAME

Trace the word plane with your finger. Color the plane.

plane

NAME

LESSON 12
WORKSHEET 57

Match the items that are the same color. The student can do this either verbally or by drawing a line.

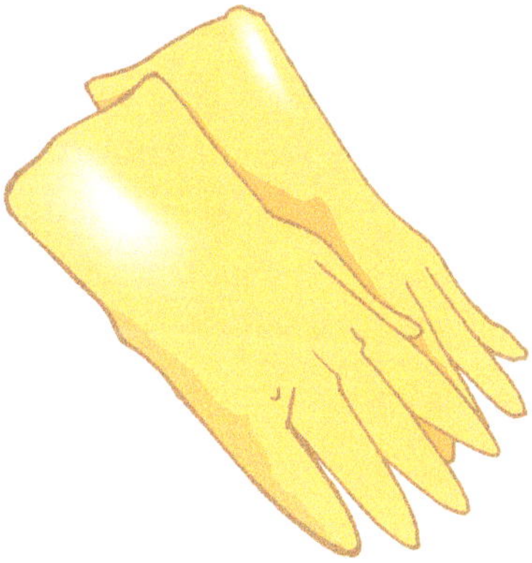
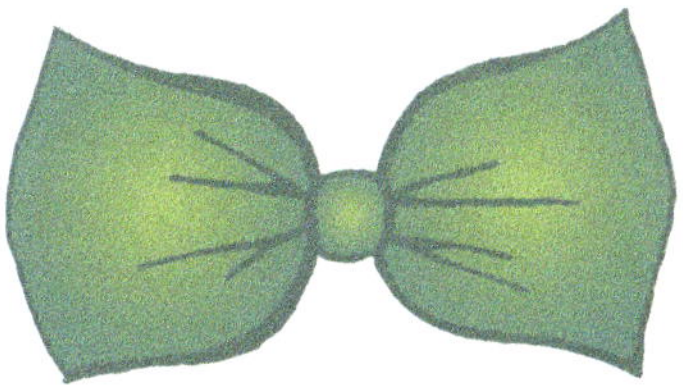
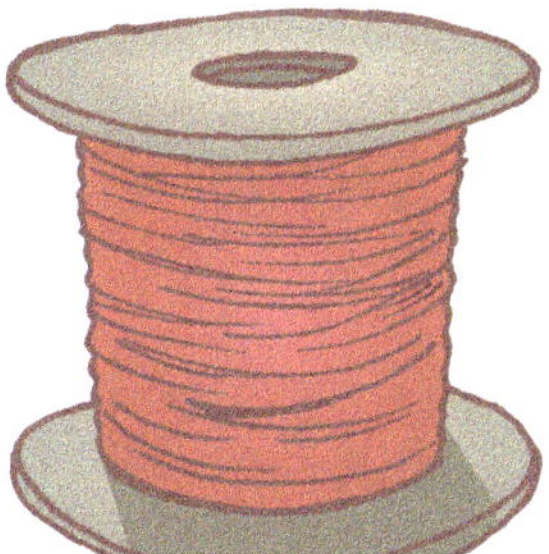

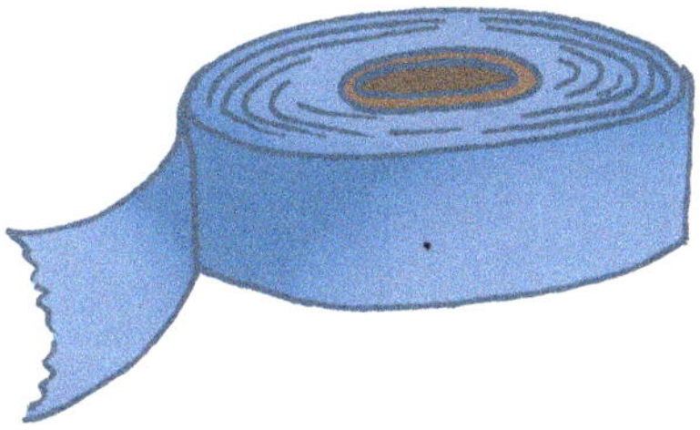

Count each group of planes. Circle the group of seven planes. Color the planes.

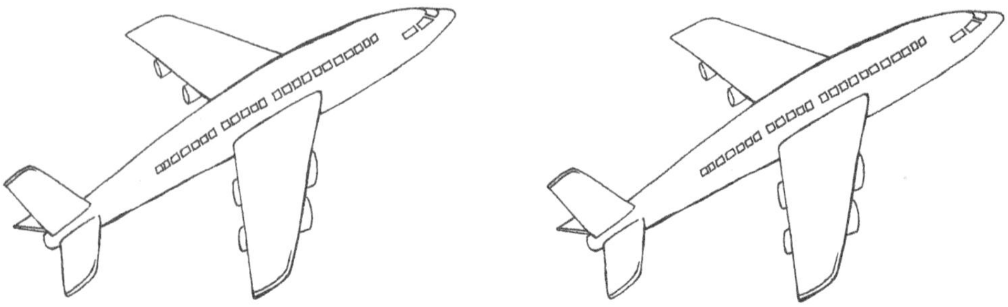

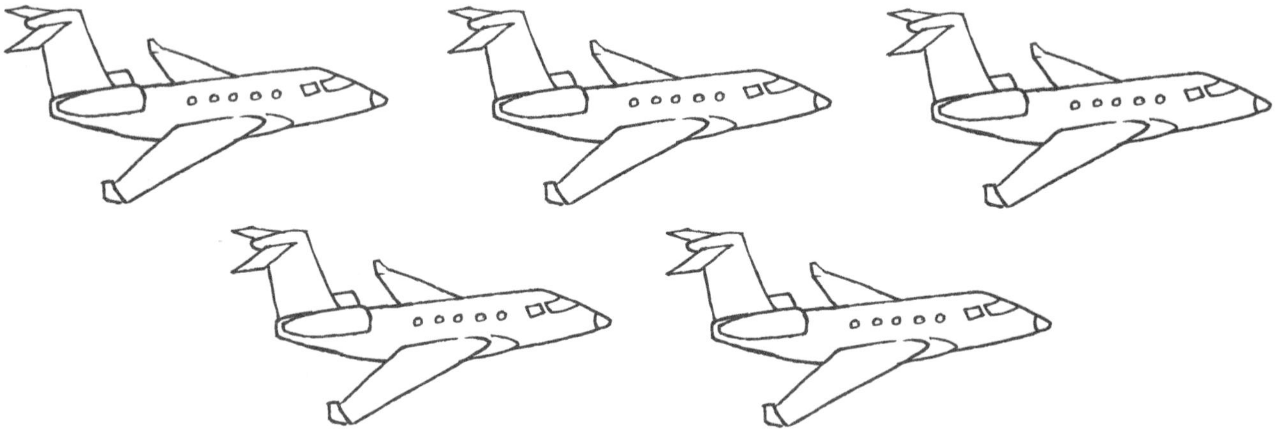

NAME

Color the DON'T WALK symbol red. Color the WALK symbol green. Color the top TRAFFIC light red, the middle light yellow, and the bottom light green.

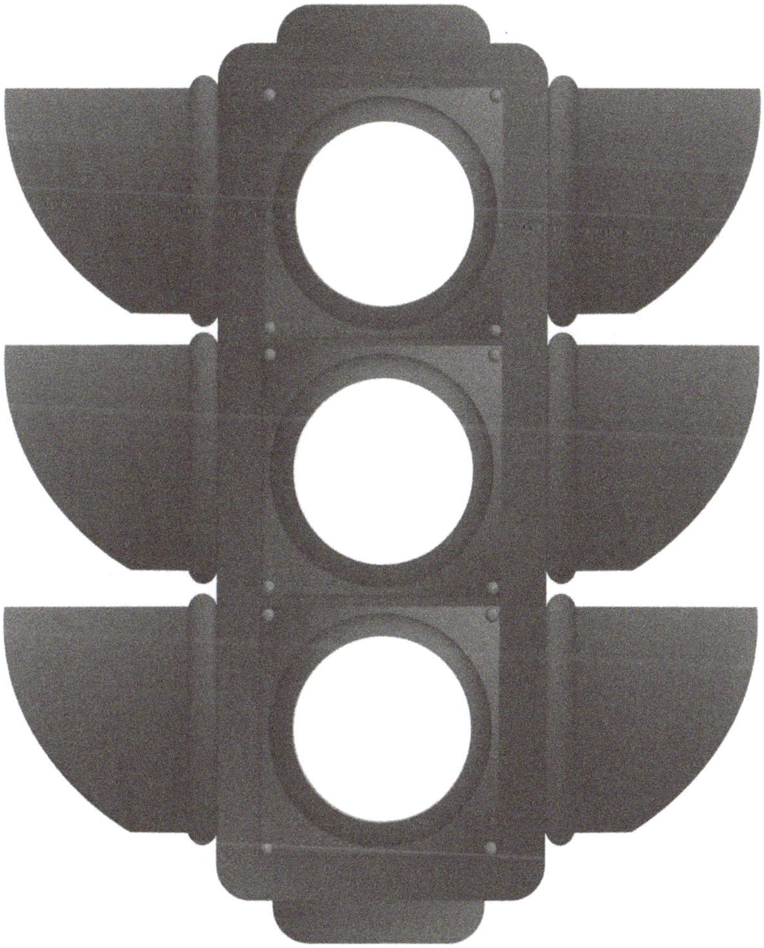

Color the car blue. Color the train green.
Color the truck red. Color the plane yellow.

NAME

Guide the student's hand as they complete the dot-to-dot, and then color the picture.

LESSON 13

WORKSHEETS 61-64

Bible Story: God Speaks to Samuel, 1 Samuel 3

NAME

Trace the word boat with your finger. Color the boat.

boat

NAME

Count the number of blue boats. Count the number of brown boats that have a red sail. Count the total number of boats.

Follow the dashed lines to draw circles.
Follow the dashed lines to draw sticks.

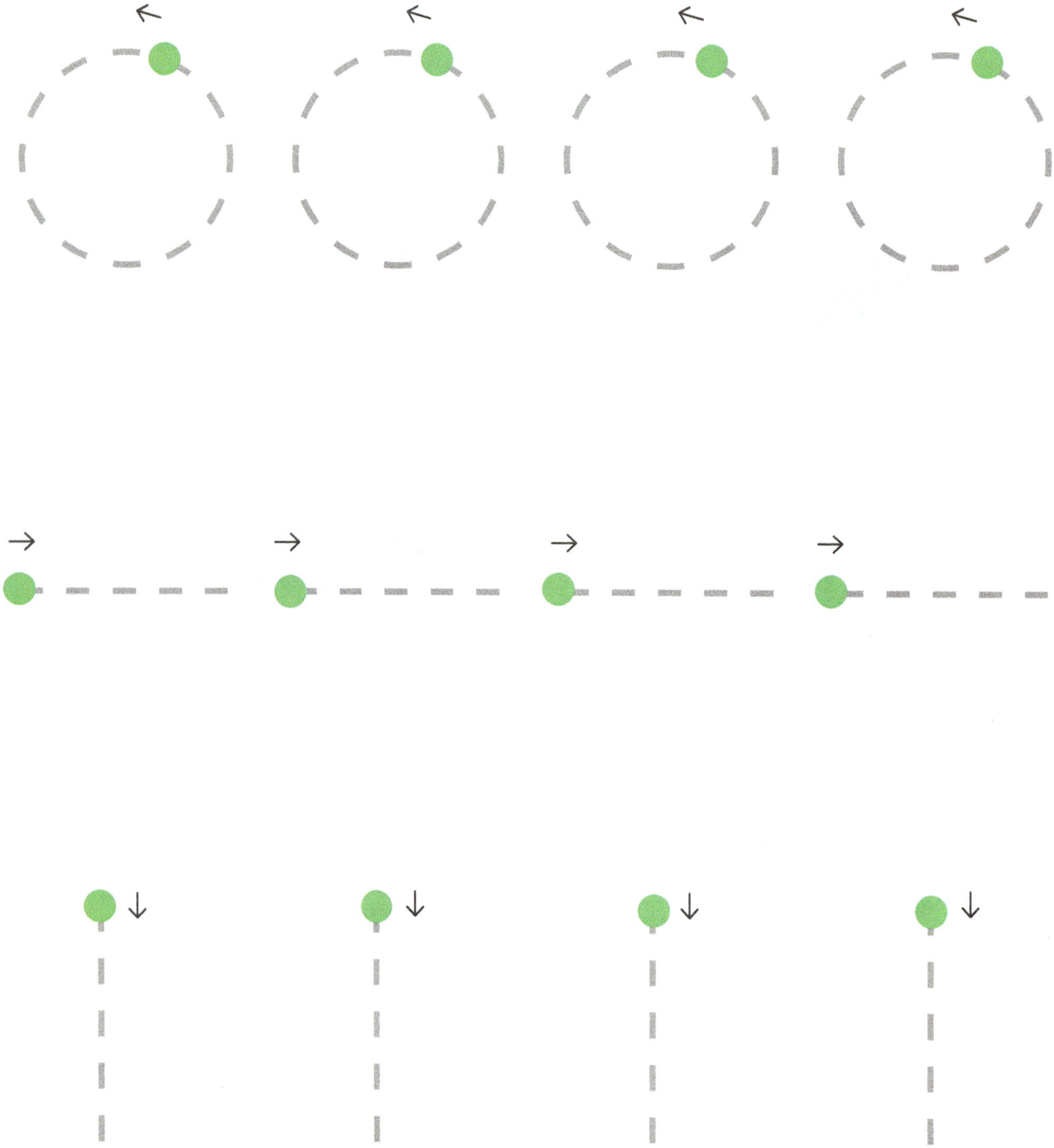

NAME

LESSON 13
WORKSHEET 63

Color the STOP sign red. Color the WALK sign yellow.
Color the person in the DON'T WALK sign black.
Color the HOSPITAL sign blue.

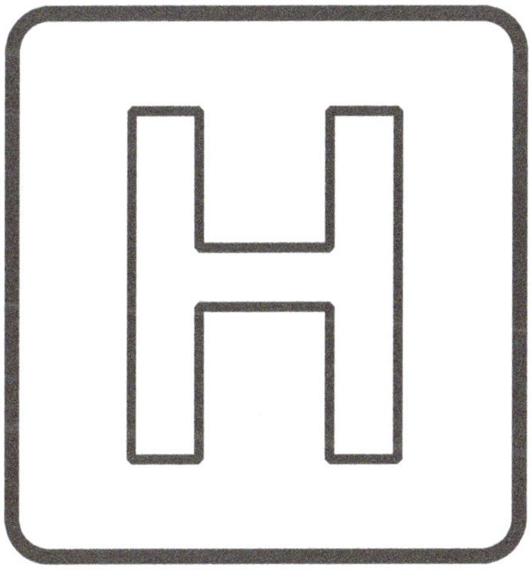

Match the baby animal to its mother.

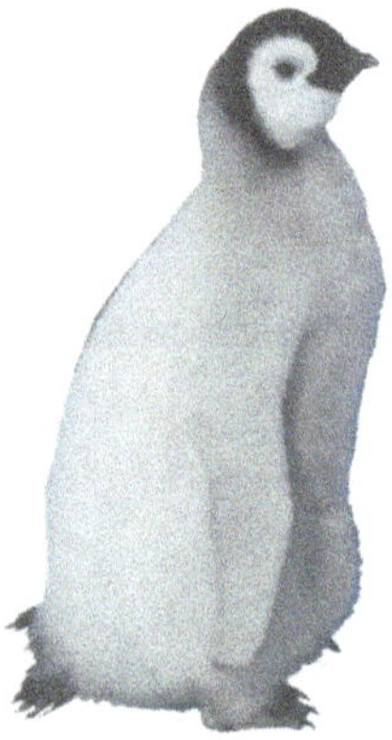

NAME

Color the pictures and then cut them apart.
Can you put them in order?

LESSON 14

WORKSHEETS 66-69

Bible Story: David and Goliath, 1 Samuel 17

NAME

Trace the word toy with your finger. Color the toy.

toy

NAME

Follow the dashed lines to draw circles.
Follow the dashed lines to draw sticks.

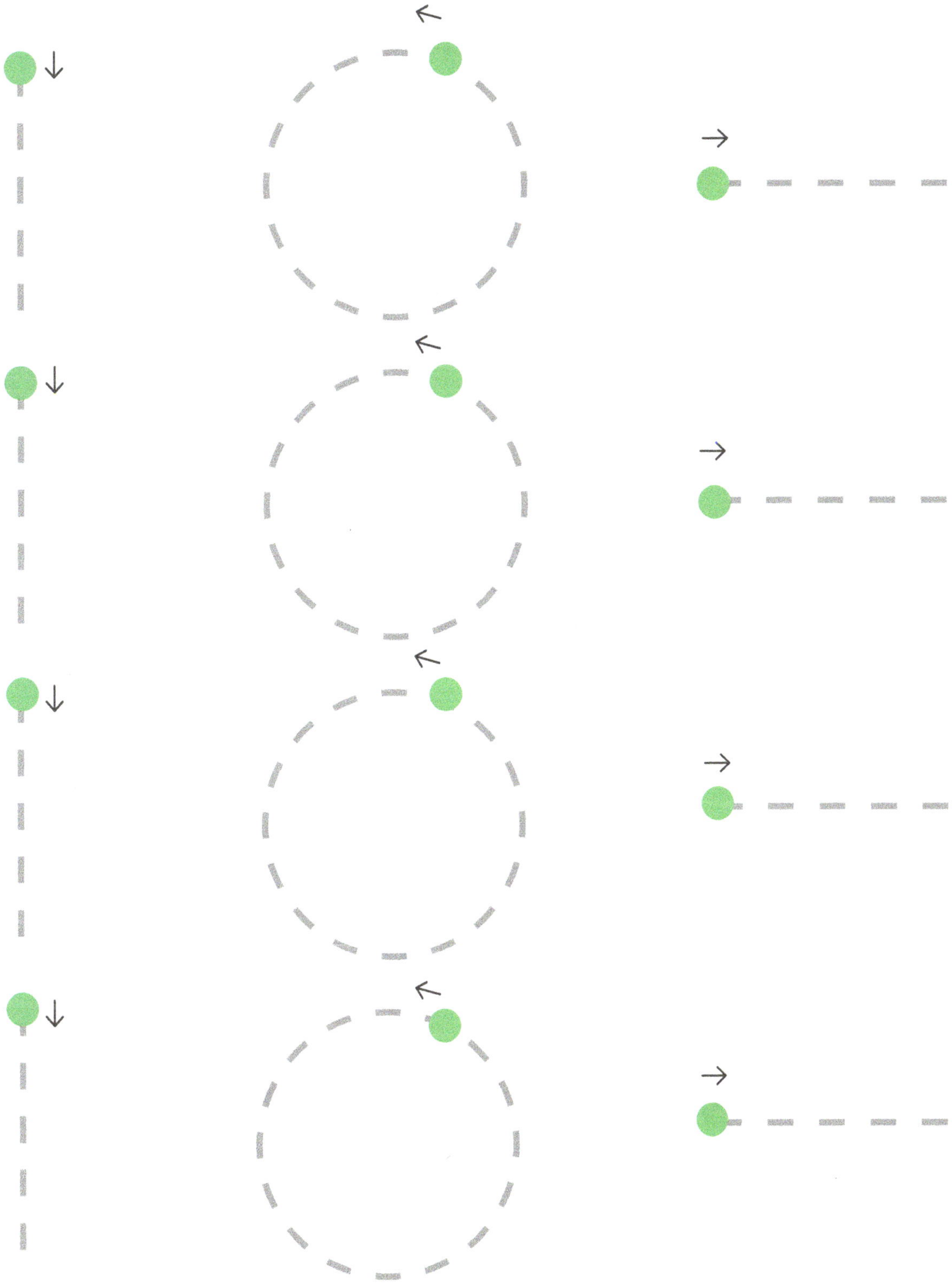

Trace the number 6. Trace the word six with your finger.
Count the toys on the page. Color the number 6.

6

six

NAME

LESSON 14
WORKSHEET 68

Circle the group of seven toys in each row.

Match the items that have the same shape.

NAME

LESSON 14
WORKSHEET 69

Count the stones that David is picking up. Color the picture.

LESSON 15

WORKSHEETS 71–74

Bible Story: David and Jonathan, 1 Samuel 20

NAME

Letter A

Trace the letters **Aa** with your finger. Color the apple.

Aa

NAME

Say the name of the item that begins with **Aa.**
Match the items.

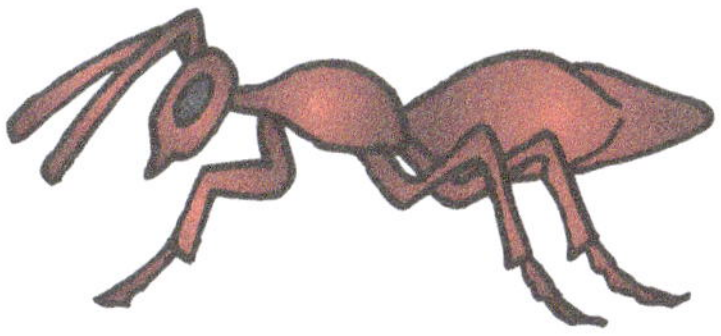

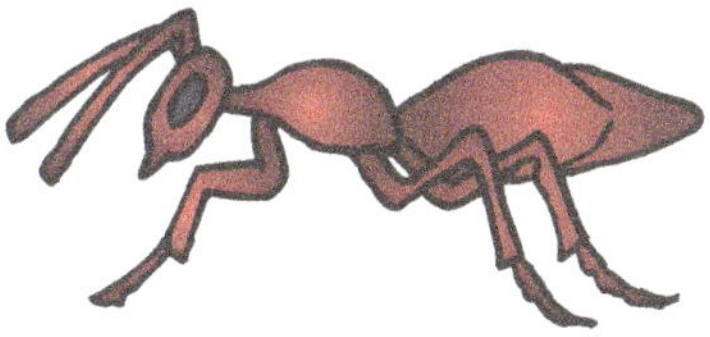

Trace five big letter **A's.**

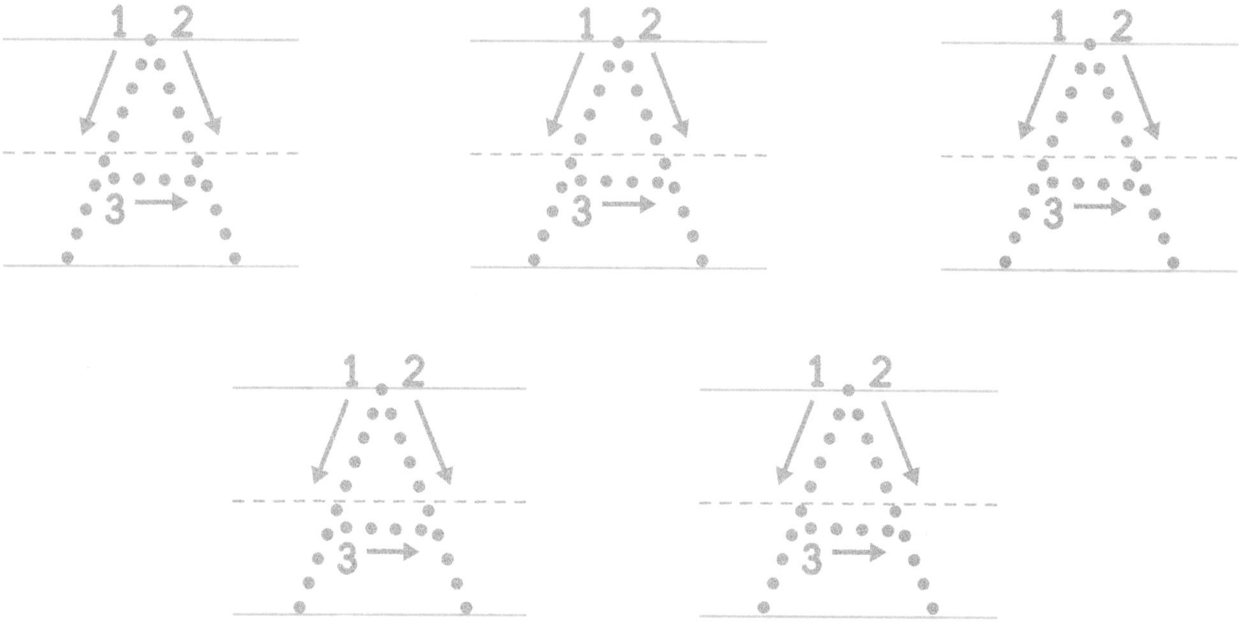

Trace five small letter **a's.**

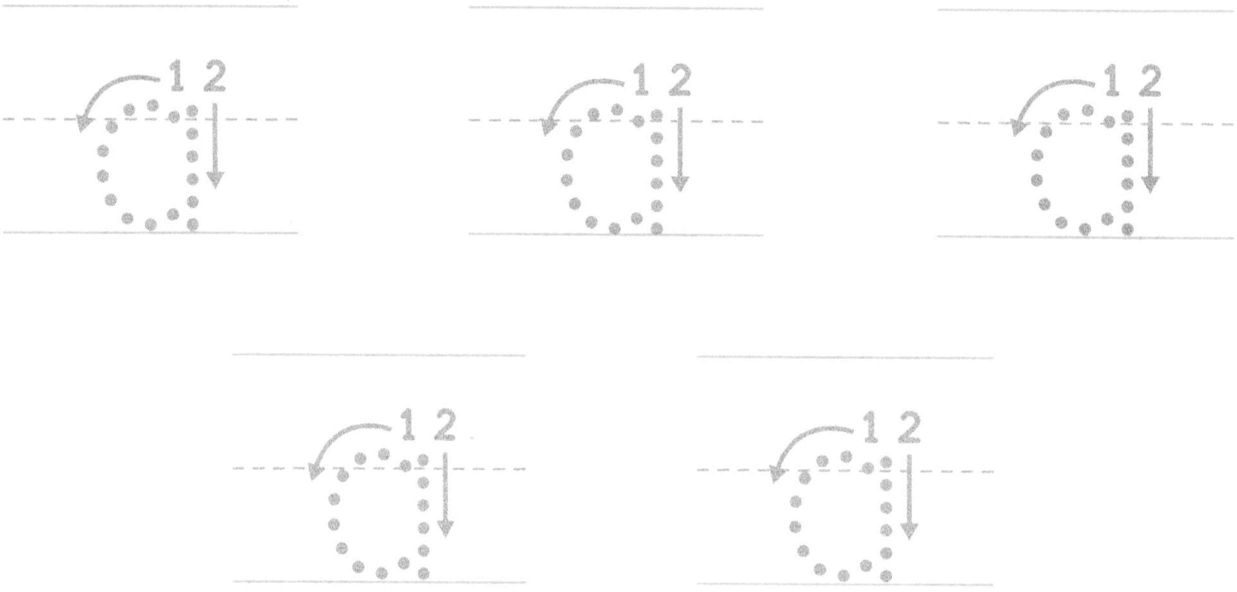

NAME

Color the circles red. Color the ovals blue. Trace two circles. Trace two ovals. Count all of the circles and ovals on the page.

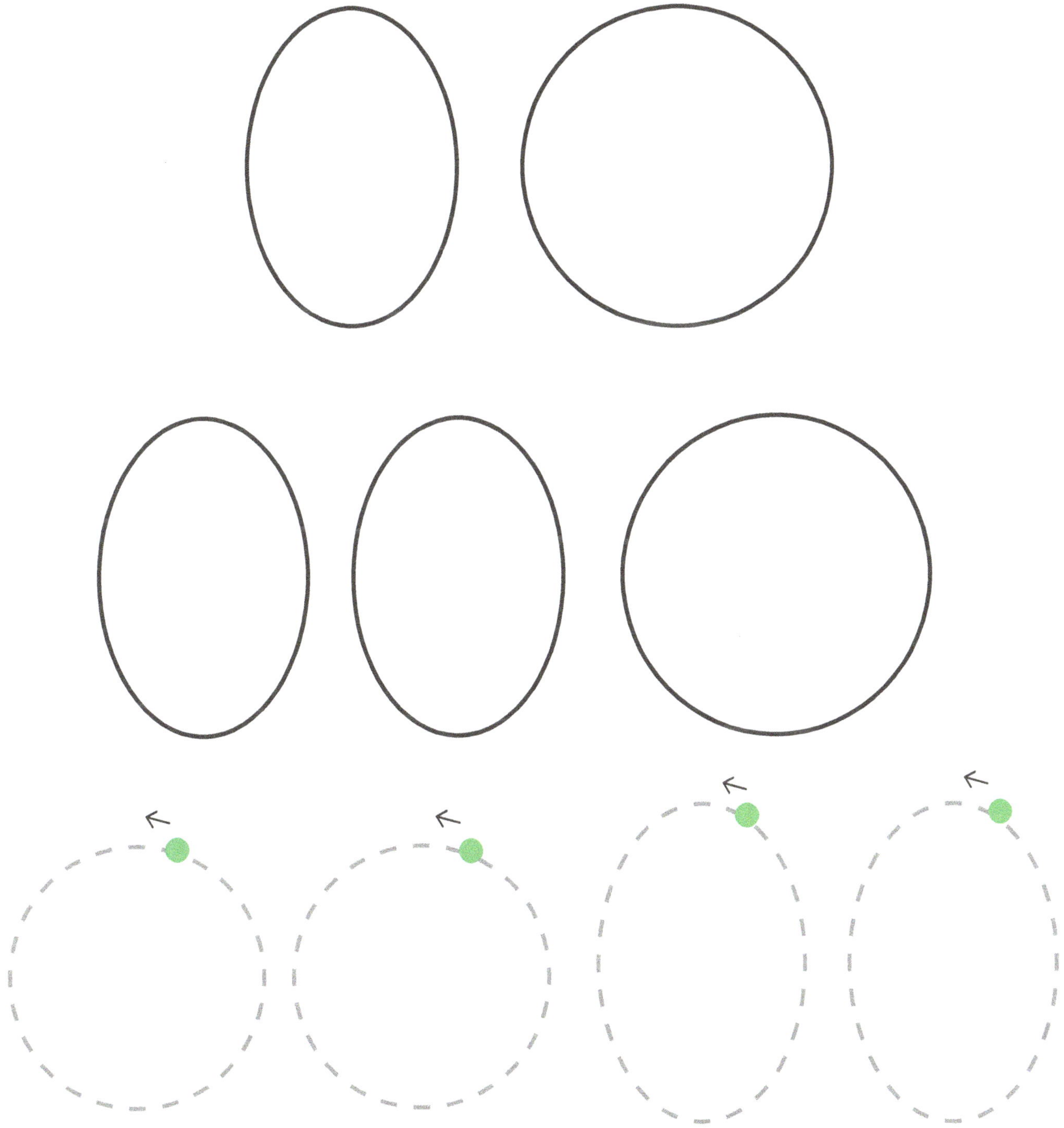

Trace the number 7. Trace the word seven with your finger.
Count the apples on the page. Count the number of red apples.
Count the number of green apples. Count the total number of apples again.
Color the number 7.

7

seven

NAME

LESSON 15
WORKSHEET 74

Help David through the maze to find his friend Jonathan.

LESSON 16

WORKSHEETS 76-79

Bible Story: David Writes Psalms, Psalm 150

NAME

Letter B

Trace the letters **Bb** with your finger. Color the butterfly.

Bb

NAME

Color the squares green. Color the rectangles yellow.

Trace five big letter **B's.**

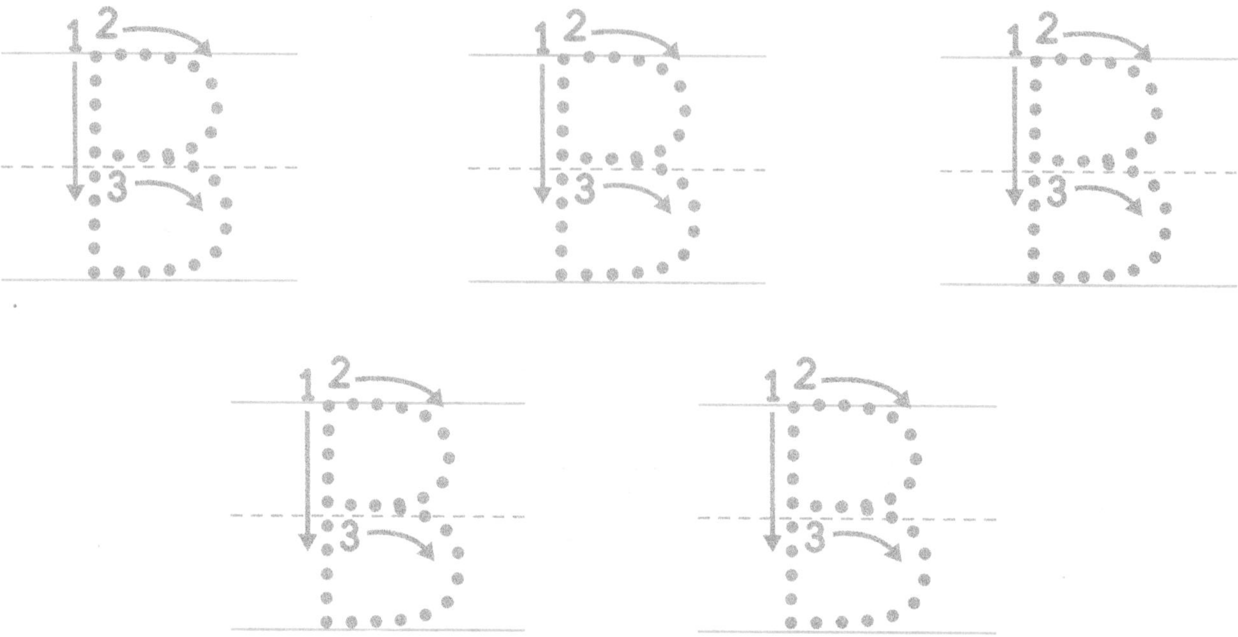

Trace five small letter **b's.**

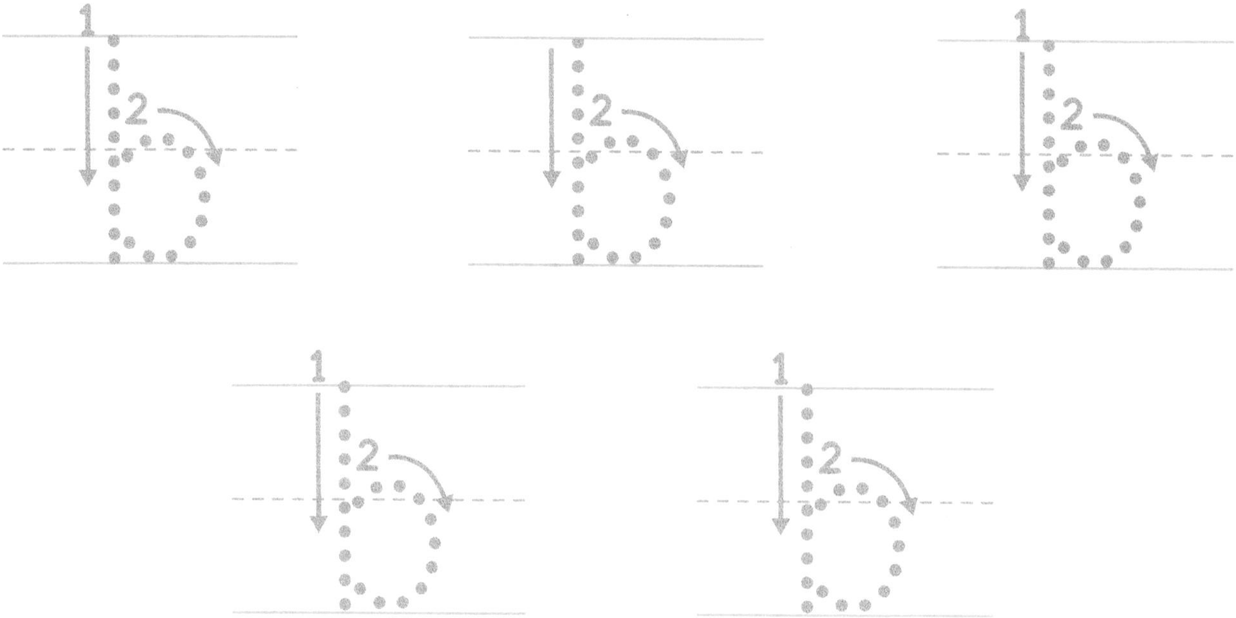

NAME

Trace the number 8. Trace the word eight with your finger.
Count the butterflies on the page. Color the number 8.

8

eight

Circle the smallest ball. Put an X over the largest ball.

Circle the smallest bike. Put an X over the largest bike.

Circle the smallest boat. Put an X over the largest boat.

NAME ______________________________

Help the student write a Praise Psalm by filling the blanks below.

________________'s Psalm of Praise to God

Praise the Lord!

Praise him with trumpet's sound,

Praise him with the sound of ______________.

Praise him when the rain falls down,

Praise him when ______________.

Praise him for the gift of flowers,

Praise him for the ________________.

Praise him for the food we eat,

Praise him for ______________________.

Praise the Lord!

LESSON 17

WORKSHEETS 81-84

Bible Story: Esther Becomes Queen, Esther 1:1-2:18

NAME

Letter C

Trace the letters **Cc** with your finger. Color the car.

Cc

NAME

LESSON 17
WORKSHEET 82

Count each group of crayons Circle the group of nine crayons. Color the crayons.

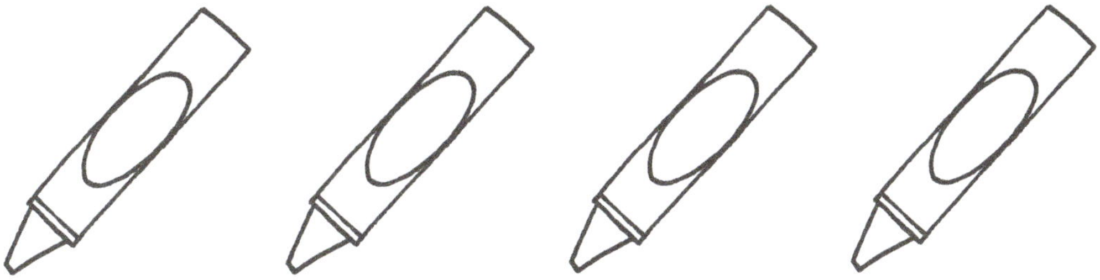

Trace five big letter **C's.**

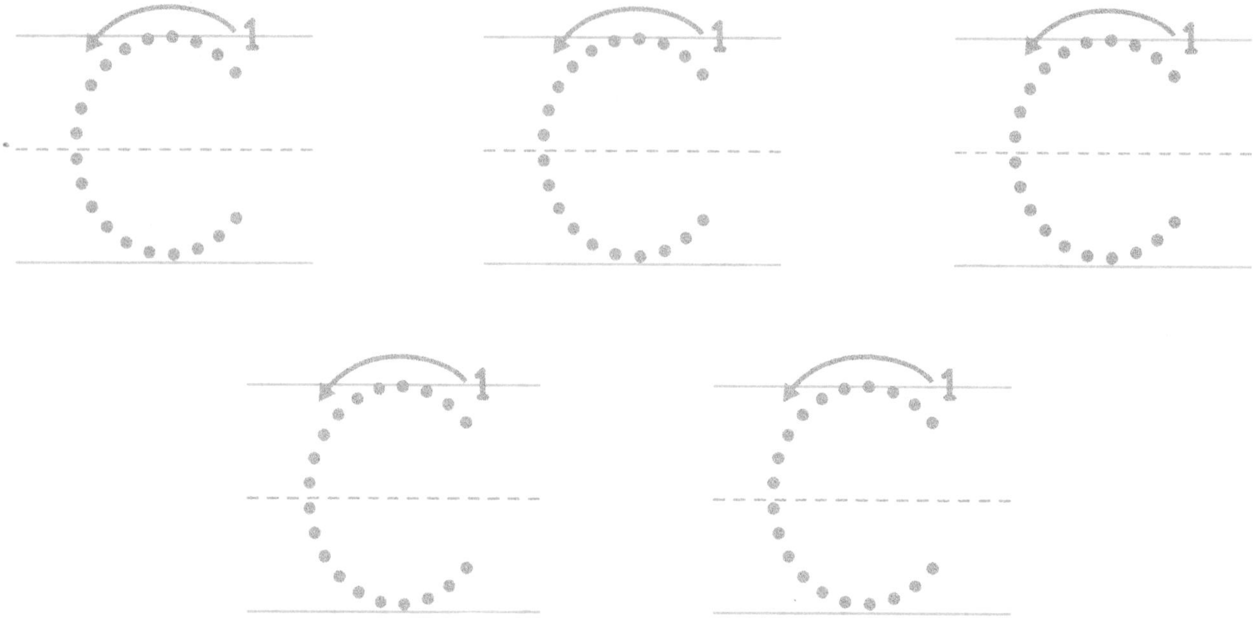

Trace five small letter **c's.**

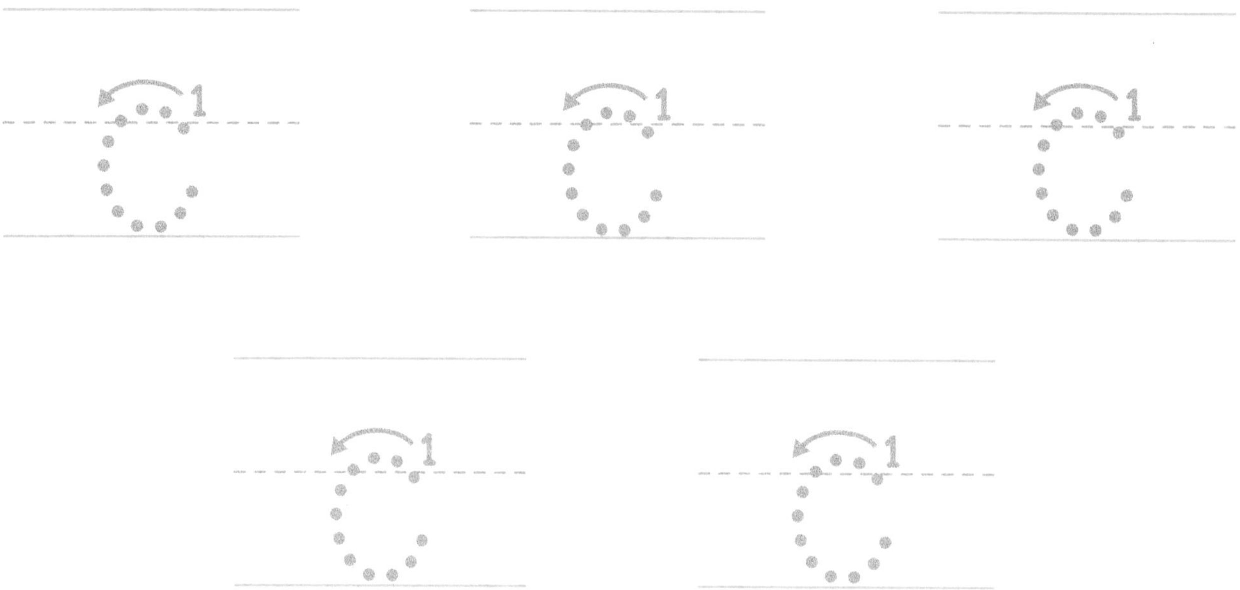

NAME

Circle the diamonds. Put an X over the triangles.

Circle the items you like to eat. Put an X on the items you don't like to eat. Is there anything that you have never tried to eat?

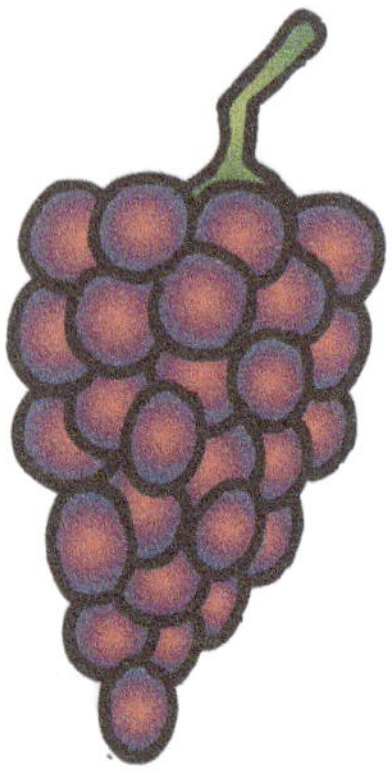

Cut out the finger puppets below and use them to retell the story of Esther.

Queen Esther

Mordecai

King Xerxes

Haman
(save for Lesson 18)

Queen Esther

Mordecai

King Xerxes

Haman

LESSON 18

WORKSHEETS 86-89

Bible Story: Esther Saves Her People, Esther 2:19-10:3

NAME

Letter D

Trace the letters **Dd** with your finger. Color the dolphin.

Dd

NAME

These animals begin with the letter **d.** Say the name of the animal.
Find each animal again in the picture at the bottom.

Trace five big letter **D's.**

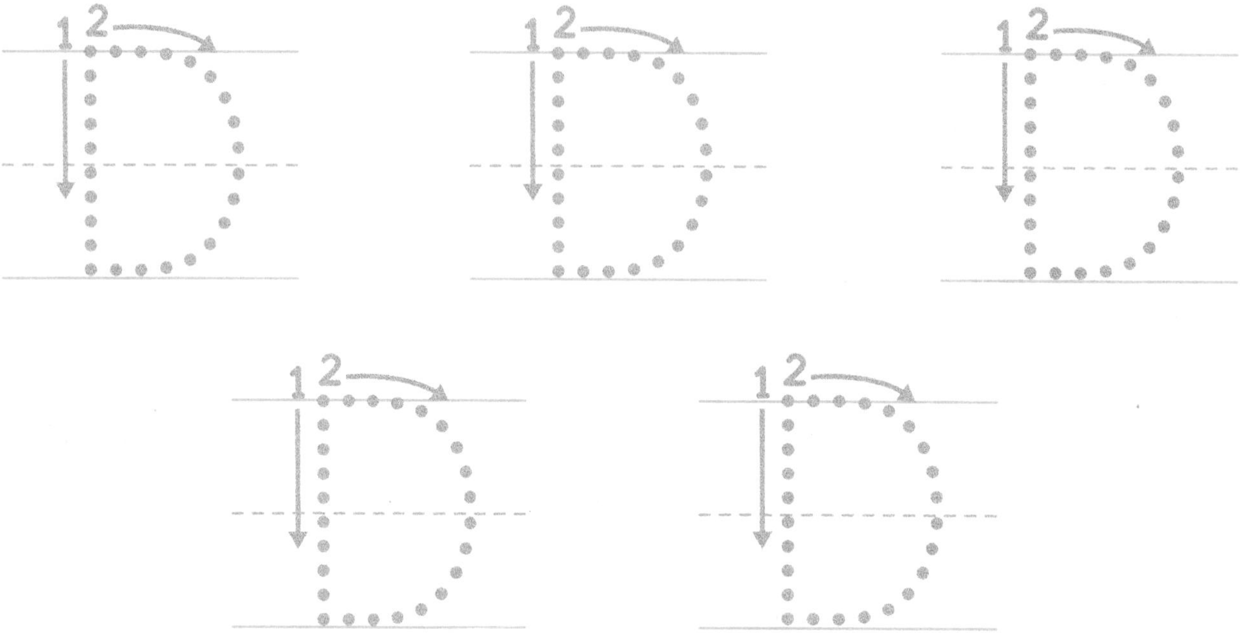

Trace five small letter **d's.**

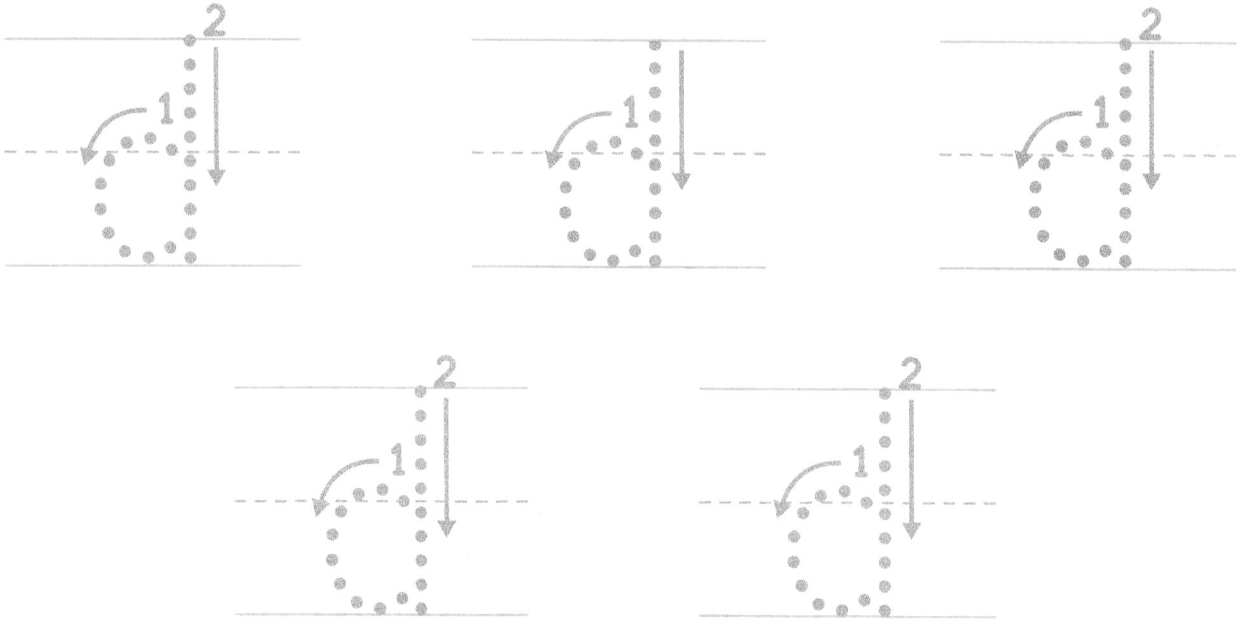

NAME

Count the number of ducks on the page. Count the number of dolphins. Count the number of dogs. Count the total number of animals.

Count each group of ducks Circle the group of ten ducks.
Color the ducks.

NAME

Connect the dots to form the crowns on Esther and the King. Color the picture.

LESSON 19

WORKSHEETS 91–94

Bible Story: Jonah and the Big Fish, Jonah 1–2

NAME

Letter E

Trace the letters **Ee** with your finger. Color the eagle.

E e

NAME

LESSON 19
WORKSHEET 92

Circle which picture should come next to complete the pattern in each row.

Trace five big letter **E's.**

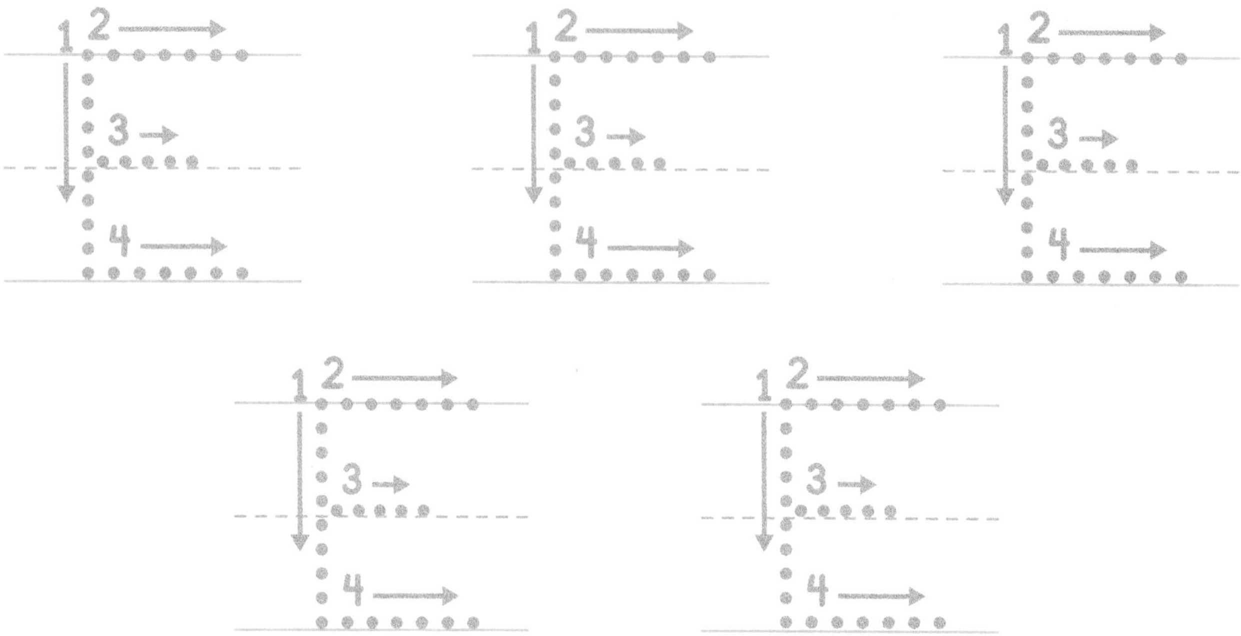

Trace five small letter **e's.**

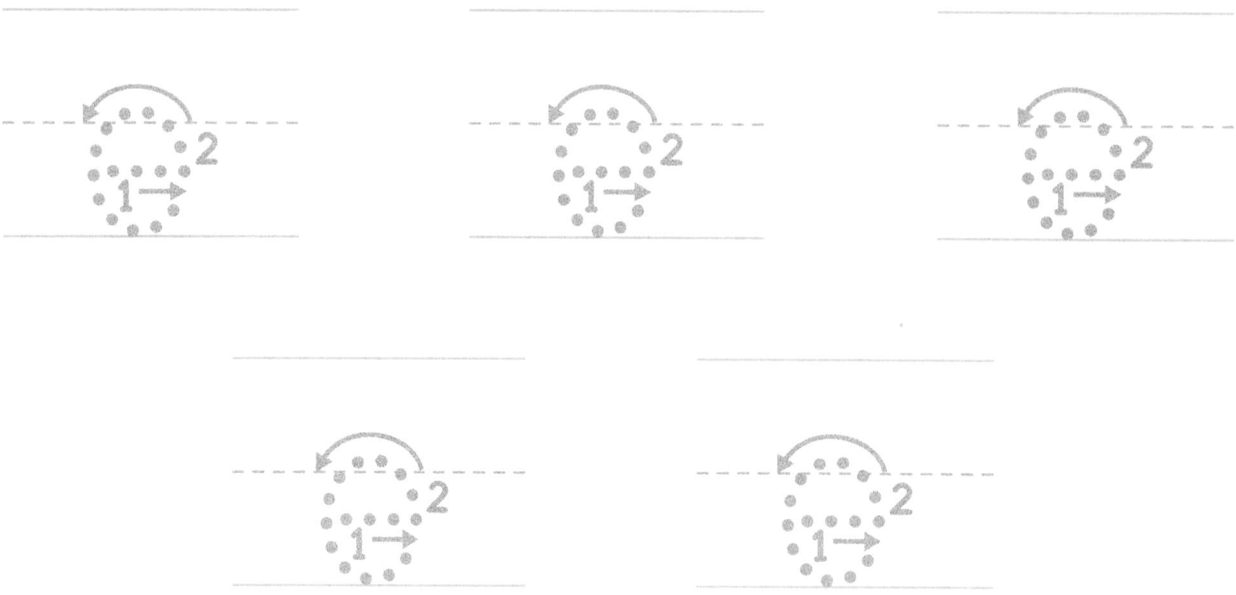

NAME

LESSON 19
WORKSHEET 93

Trace the number 9. Trace the word nine with your finger.
Count the eggs on the page. Color the number 9.

9

nine

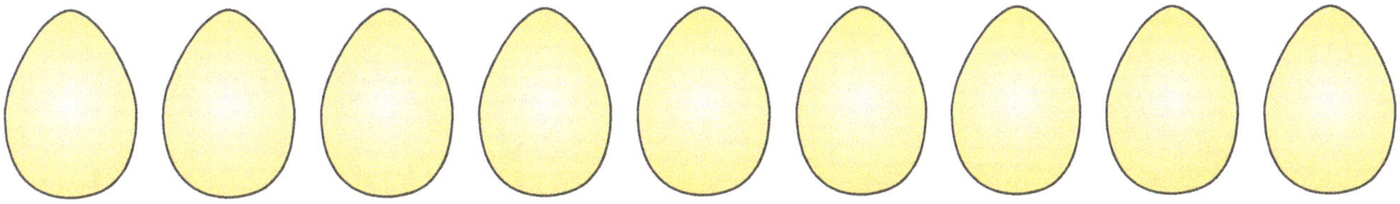

Circle the picture with nine items in each row.

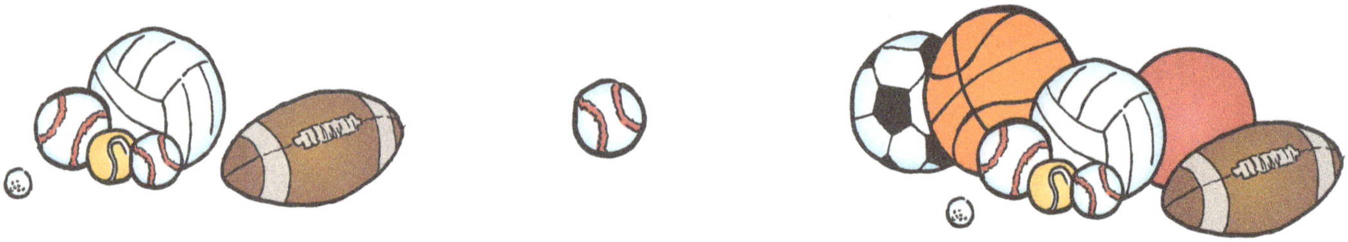

NAME

LESSON 19
WORKSHEET 94

Draw a storm like the one Jonah saw and felt.

LESSON 20

WORKSHEETS 96–99

Bible Story: Jonah Preaches in Nineveh, Jonah 3–4

NAME

Letter F

Trace the letters **Ff** with your finger. Color the flower.

Ff

NAME

LESSON 20
WORKSHEET 97

Trace the number **10**. Trace the word ten with your finger.
Count the frogs on the page. Color the number **10**.

10

ten

Trace five big letter **F's.**

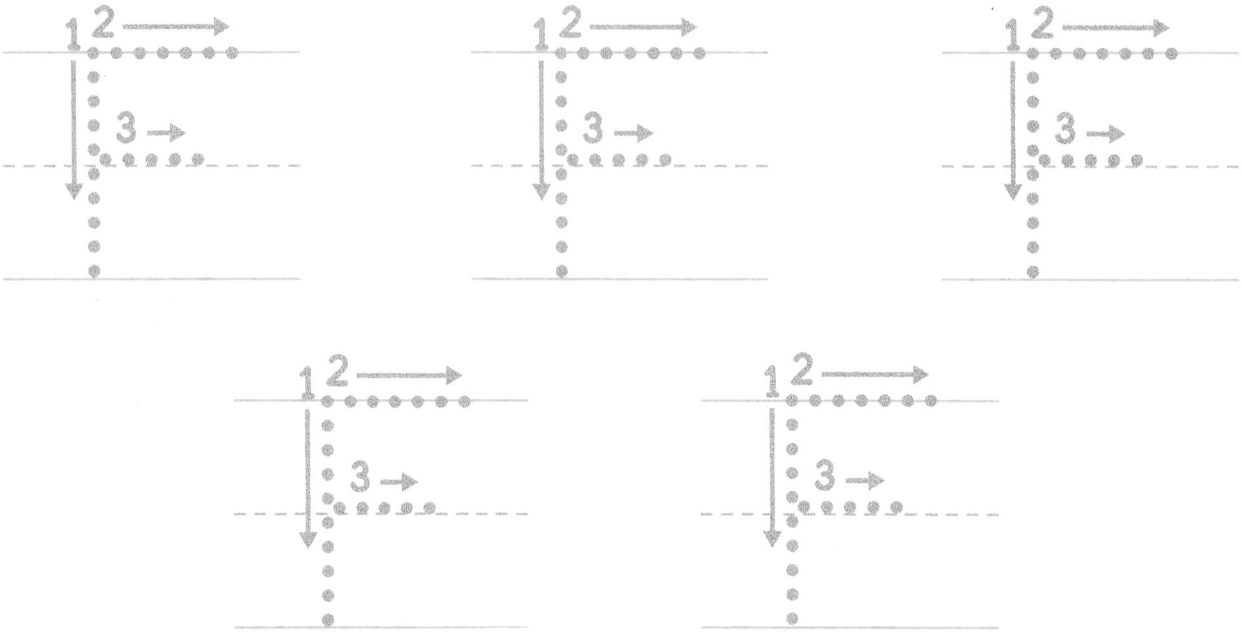

Trace five small letter **f's.**

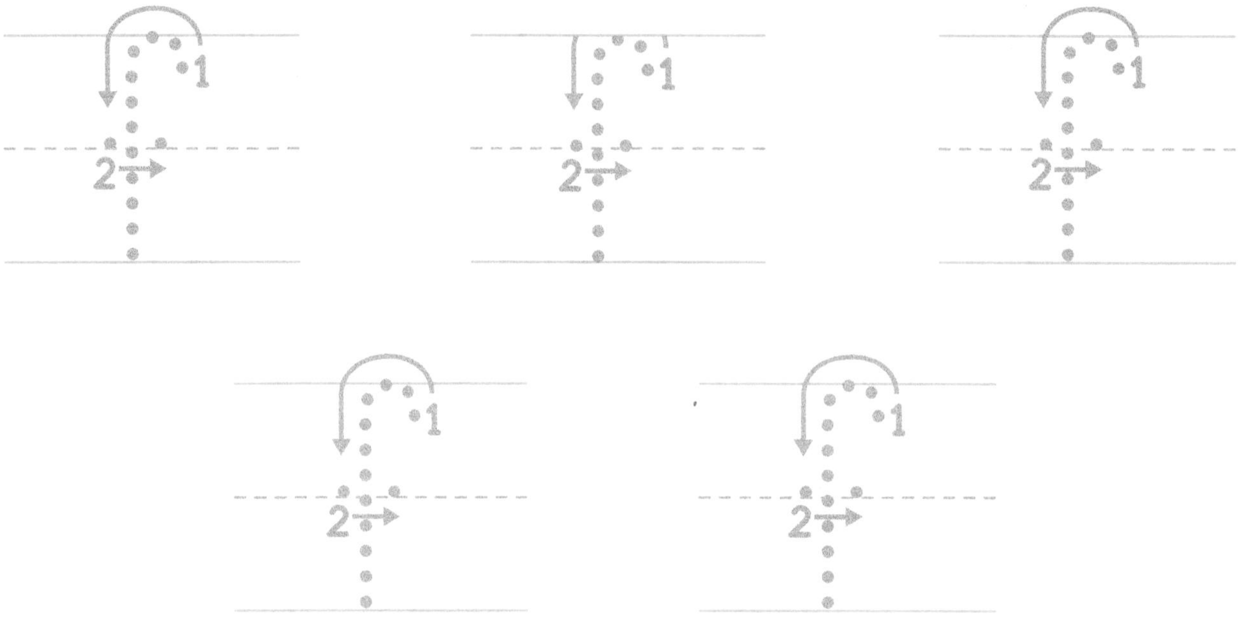

NAME

LESSON 20
WORKSHEET 98

Count each type of flower. Count the total number of flowers.

Circle which picture should come next in each line to complete the pattern.

NAME

Circle the pictures of children obeying or helping their parents. Put an X on the pictures of children who are disobedient or naughty.

LESSON 21

WORKSHEETS 101-104

Bible Story: Jesus' Birth, Luke 2:1-7

LESSON 21
WORKSHEET 101

NAME

Letter G

Trace the letters **Gg** with your finger. Color the goat.

Gg

NAME

LESSON 21
WORKSHEET 102

Count the number of items in each group.

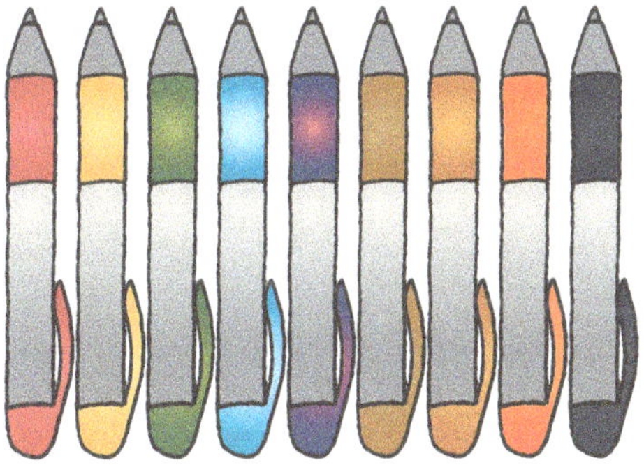

Trace five big letter **G's.**

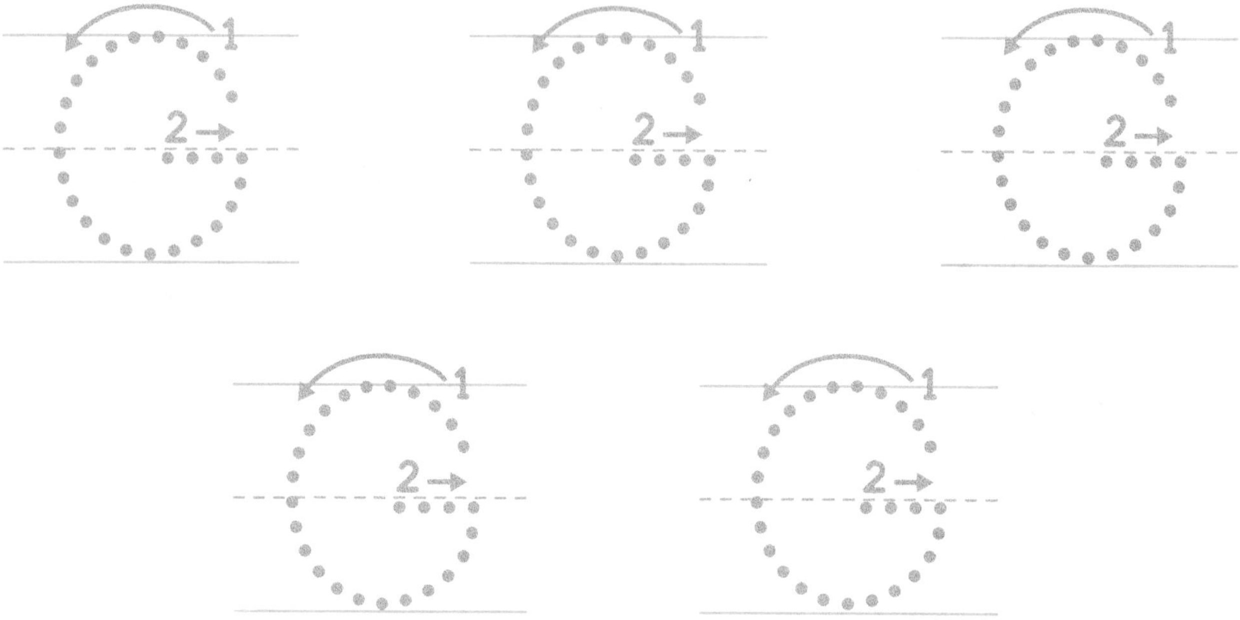

Trace five small letter **g's.**

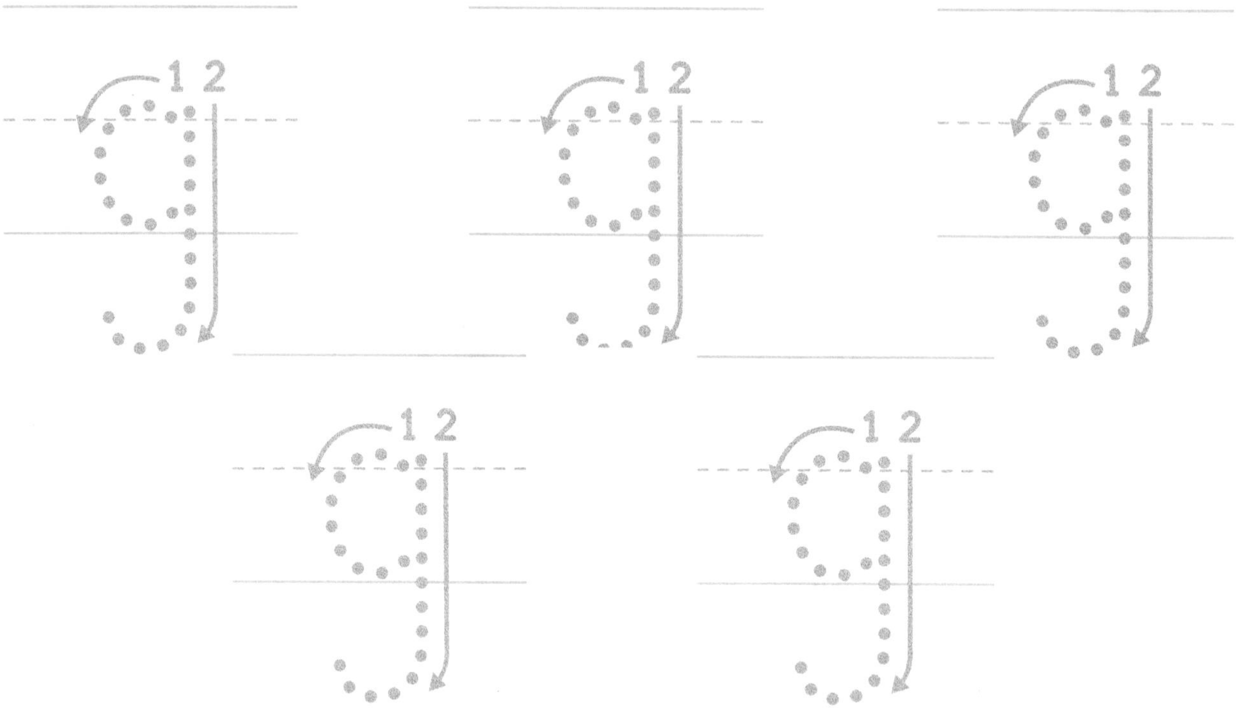

NAME

LESSON 21
WORKSHEET 103

Draw a line between the opposite items.

Color the items on the page that are smaller than a car.

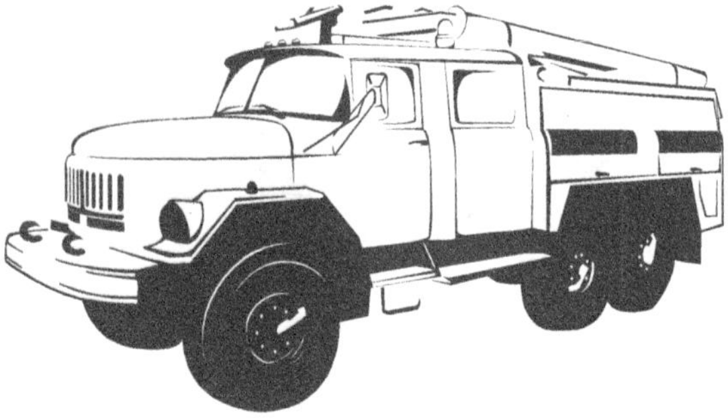

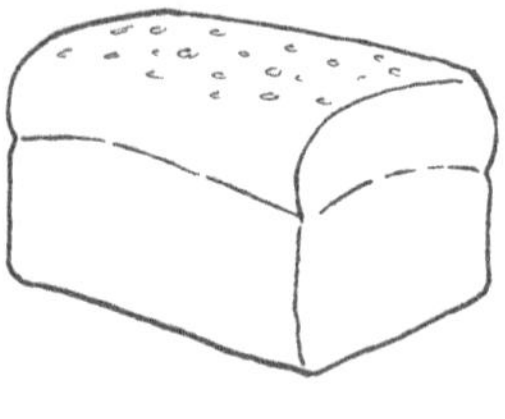

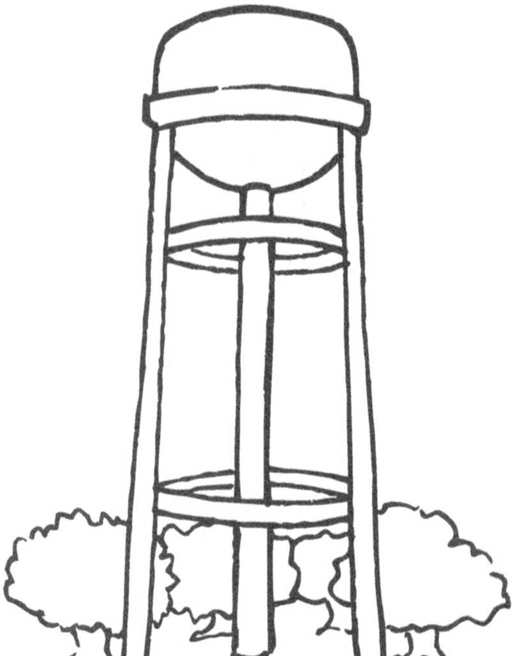

NAME

Cut out the pictures. Place the picture of baby Jesus in the hands of Mary and Joseph. Then place it in the manger. Talk about how God gave Jesus parents to care for him.

LESSON 22

WORKSHEETS 106-109

Bible Story: The Shepherds Visit Jesus, Luke 2:8-20

NAME

Letter H

Trace the letters **Hh** with your finger. Color the hen.

Hh

NAME

LESSON 22
WORKSHEET 107

Circle the object which is alive in each row.

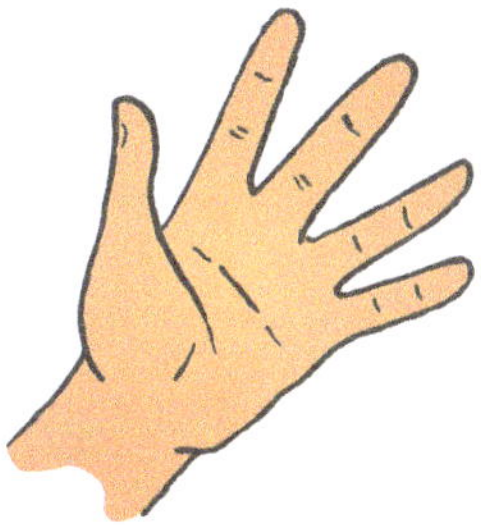

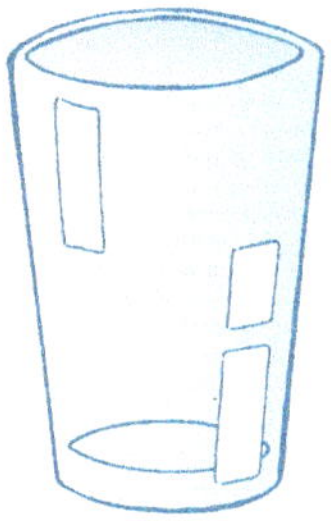

Trace five big letter **H's.**

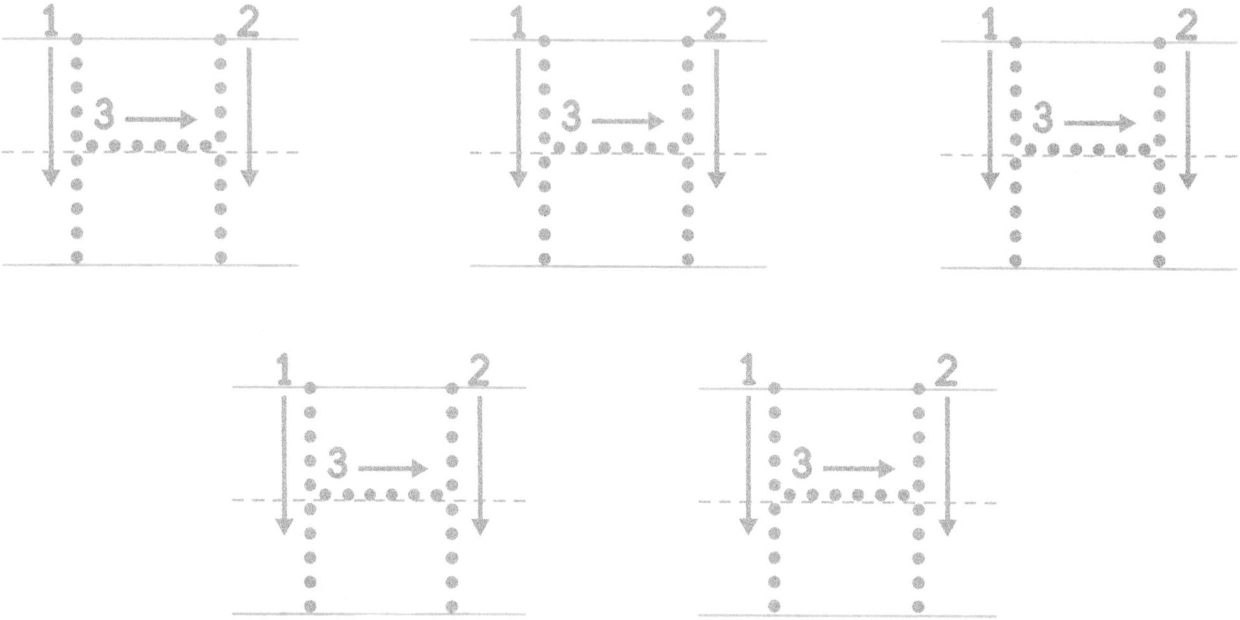

Trace five small letter **h's.**

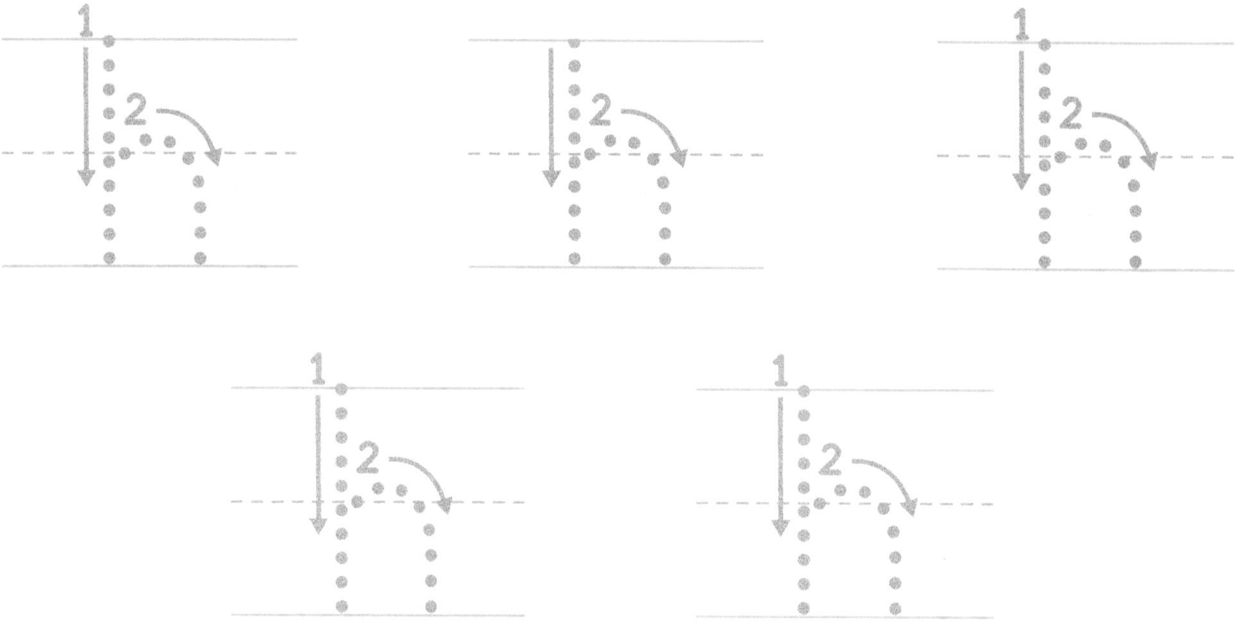

NAME

LESSON 22
WORKSHEET 108

Draw a line between the animal and its shadow.

Color the items on the page which are larger than a chair.

NAME

Look at the pictures on the side of the page. Find a shepherd's crook, a star, a sandal, a palm tree, and a mouse in the picture.

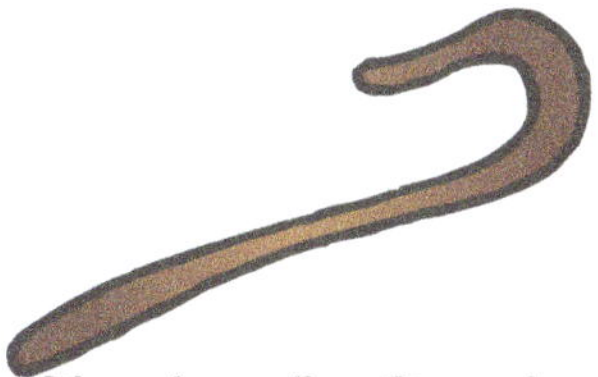

Shepherd's Crook

Star

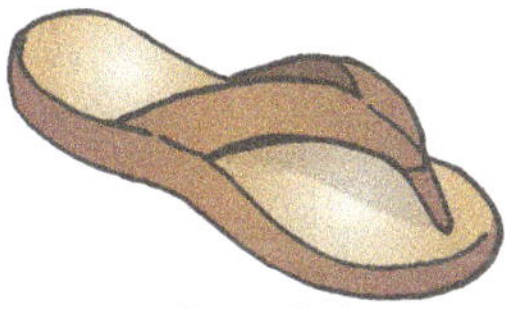

Sandal

Palm Tree

Mouse

Draw a line matching the numbers that are the same.

1	3
2	1
3	2
4	5
5	4

LESSON 23

WORKSHEETS 111-114

Bible Story: The Wise Men, Matthew 2:1-12

NAME

Letter I

Trace the letters **Ii** with your finger. Color the ice cream cone.

Ii

NAME ______________________

LESSON 23
WORKSHEET 112

Draw a line matching the number with the number of ice cream scoops.

1

2

3

4

5

Trace five big letter **I's.**

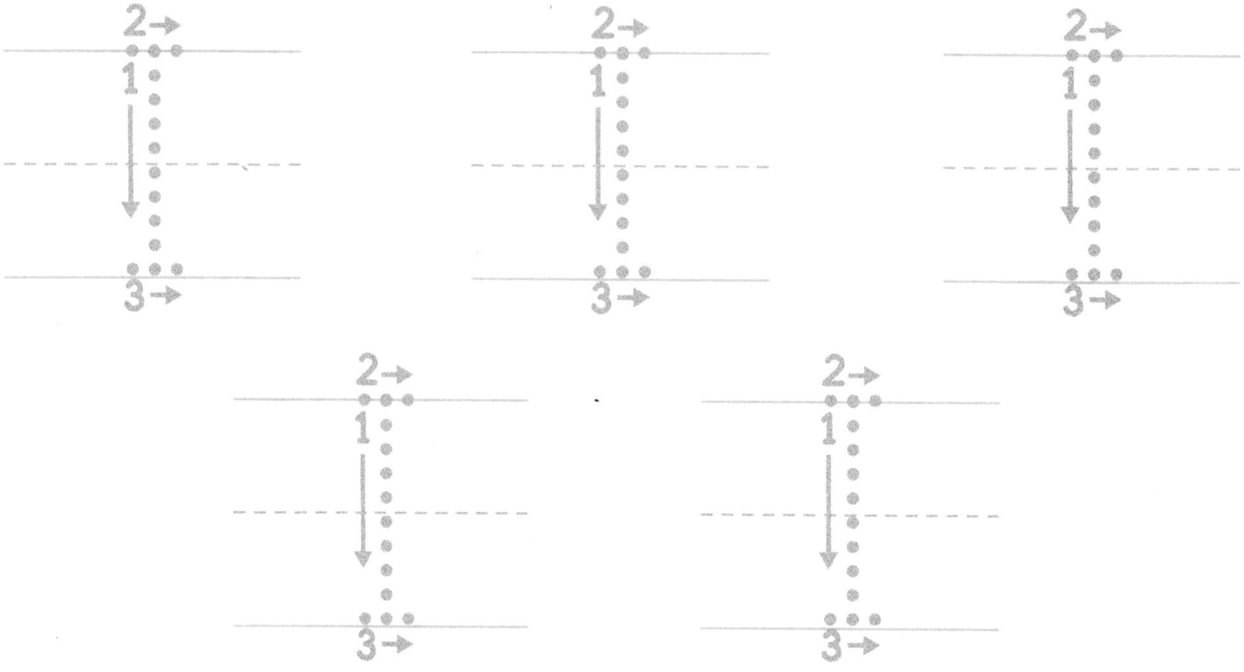

Trace five small letter **i's.**

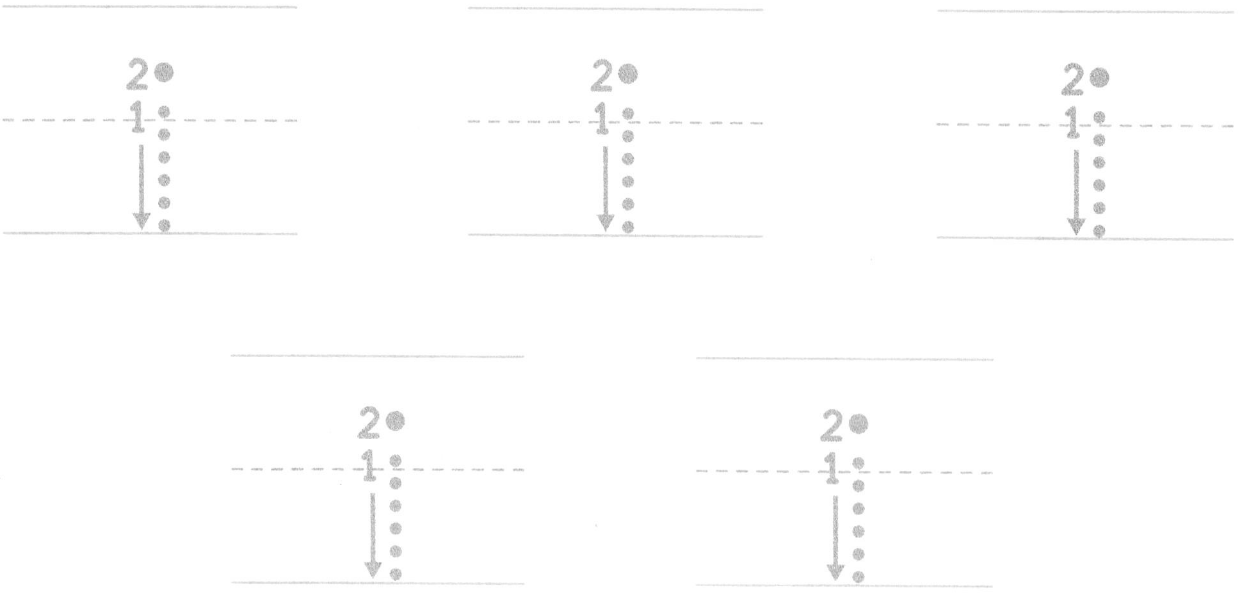

NAME

LESSON 23
WORKSHEET 113

Circle the items that are hot. Put an X on the items that are cold.

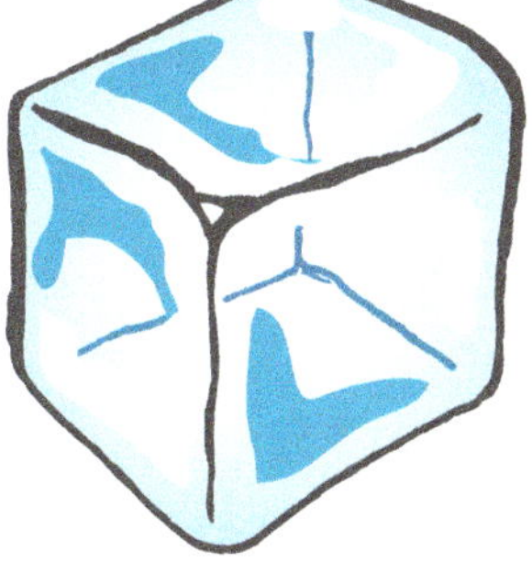

Trace the lines.

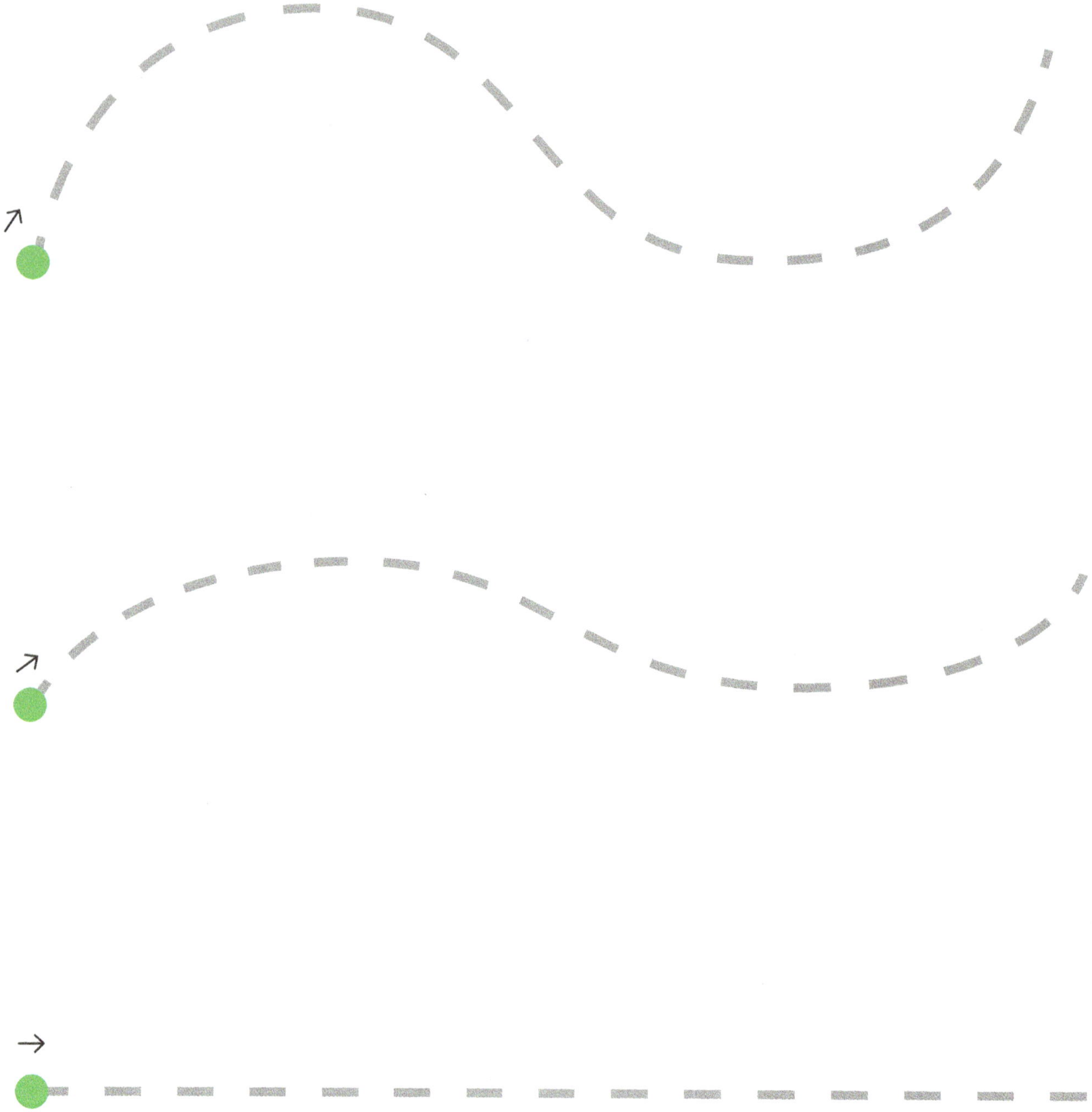

NAME

Help the wise men through the maze to find the star and baby Jesus.

Draw a line matching the numbers that are the same.

6	10
7	6
8	7
9	8
10	9

LESSON 24

WORKSHEETS 116-119

Bible Story: Jesus Calls the Disciples, Luke 5:1-11, 5:27-28, 6:12-16

NAME

Letter J

Trace the letters **Jj** with your finger. Color the jaguar.

J j

NAME

LESSON 24
WORKSHEET 117

Count the number of jelly beans in each group and match it to the correct number.

6

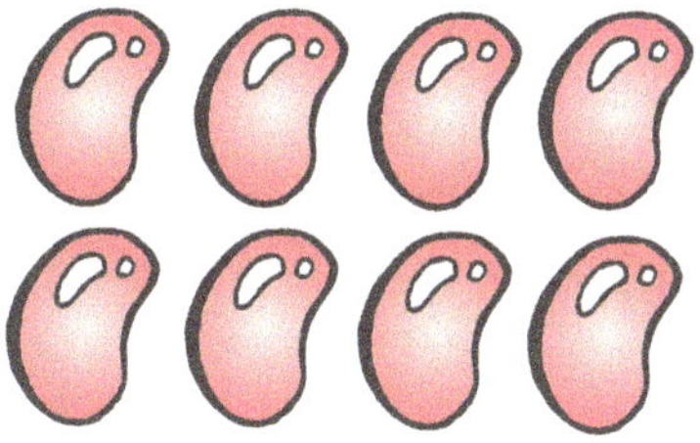

7

8

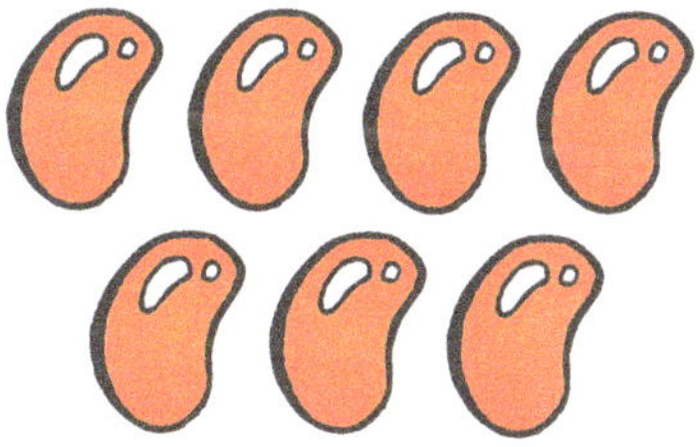

9

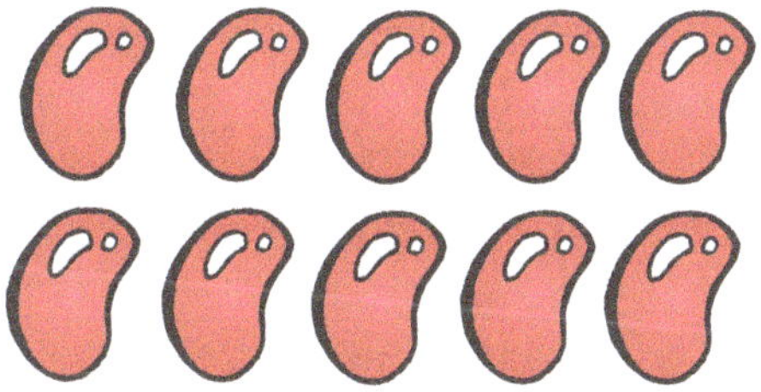

10

Trace five big letter **J's.**

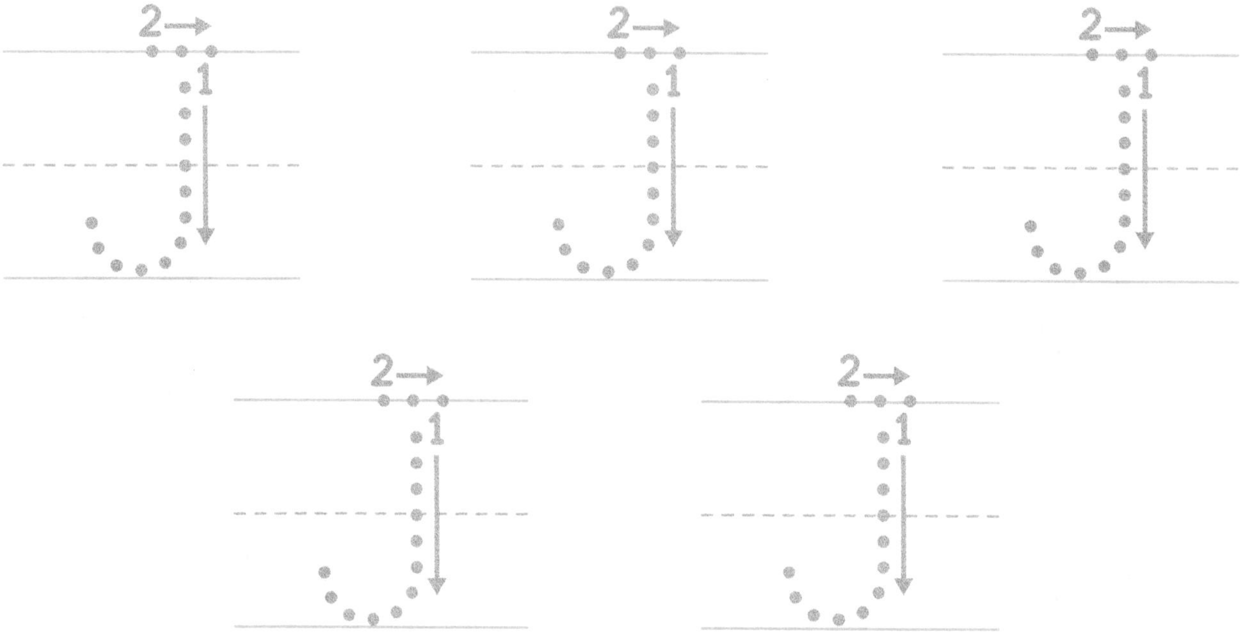

Trace five small letter **j's.**

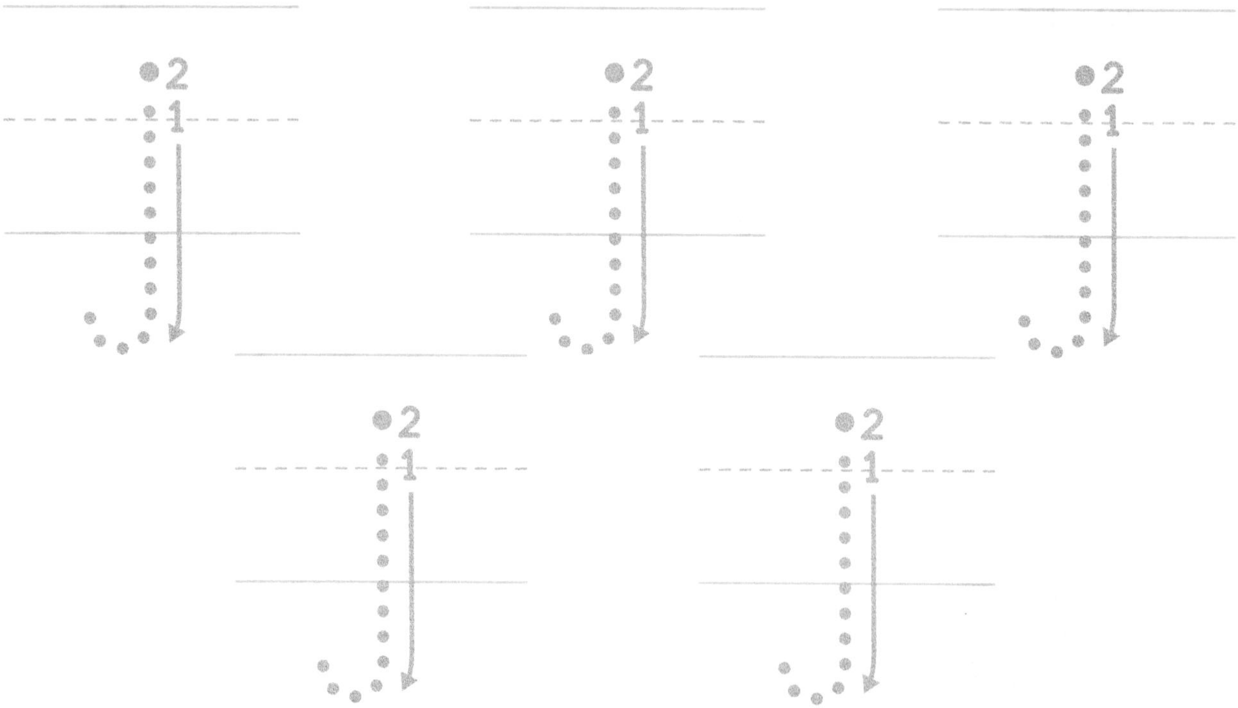

NAME

LESSON 24
WORKSHEET 118

Circle the pictures where people are happy.

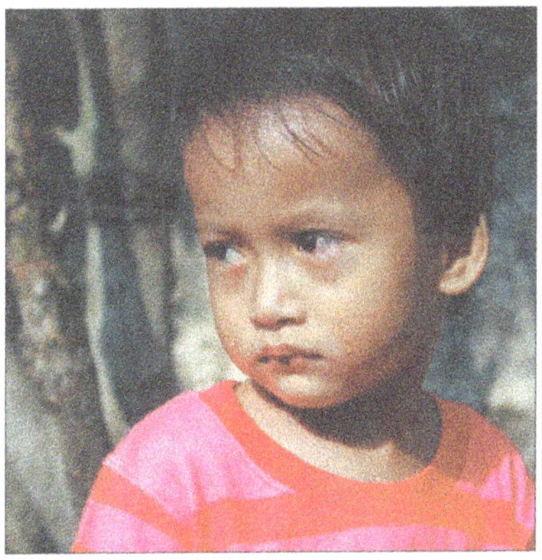

Draw the shapes by following the dotted lines.

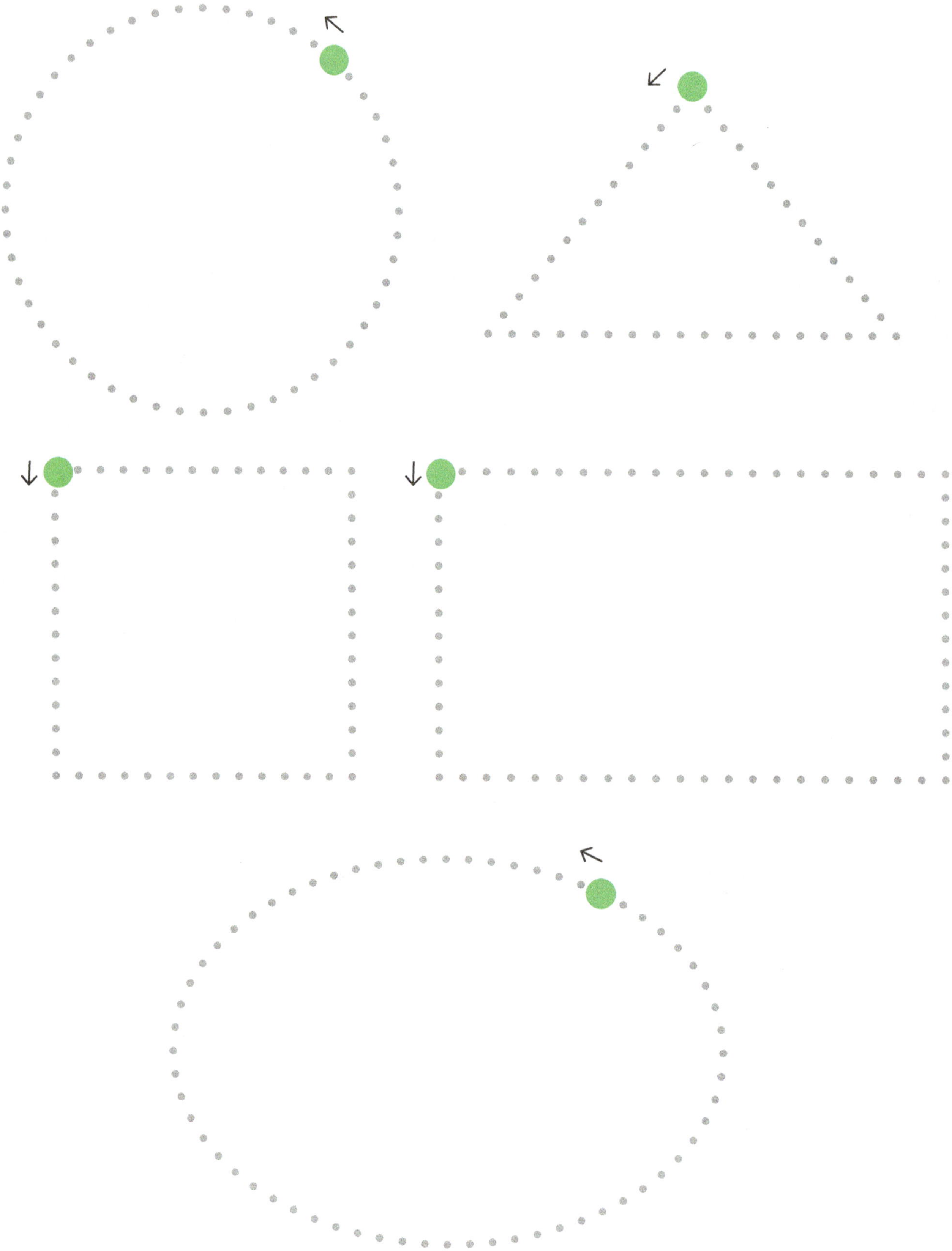

NAME

Cut the images apart. Place the pictures in the order that they happened.

LESSON 25

WORKSHEETS 121-124

Bible Story: Lame Man Through the Roof, Mark 2:1-12

LESSON 25
WORKSHEET 121

NAME

Letter K

Trace the letters **Kk** with your finger. Color the kangaroos.

Kk

NAME

LESSON 25
WORKSHEET 122

Count the number of kites in each group and match it to the correct number.

1 

2 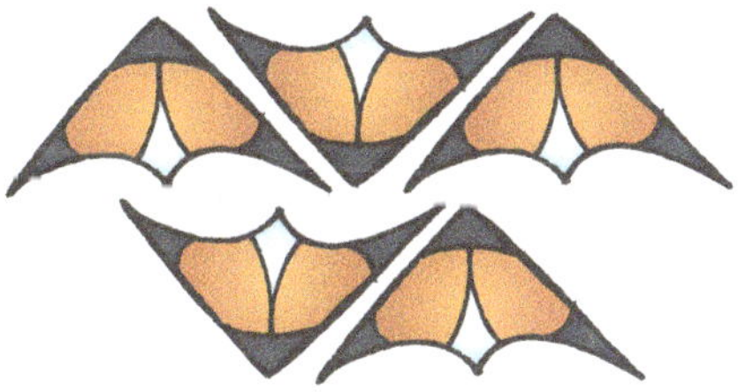

3 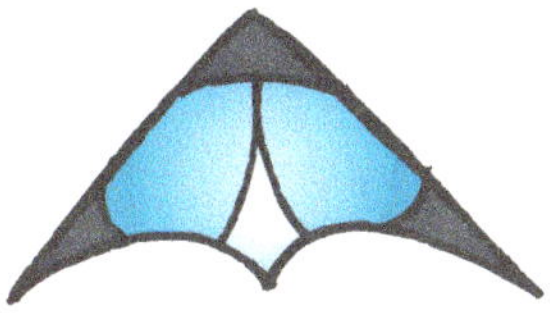

4 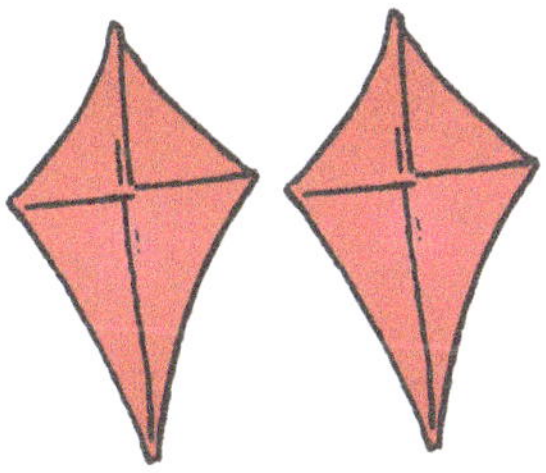

5 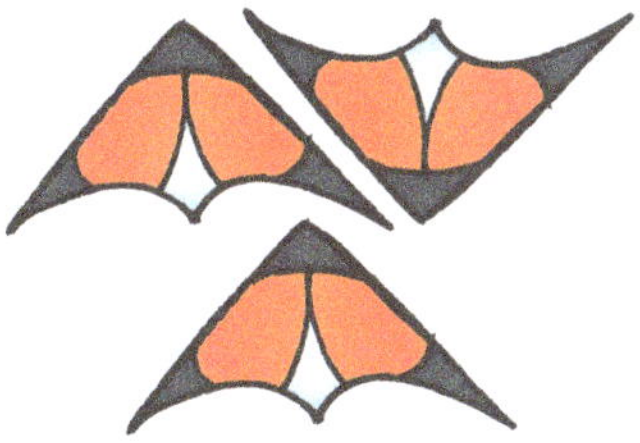

Trace five big letter **K's.**

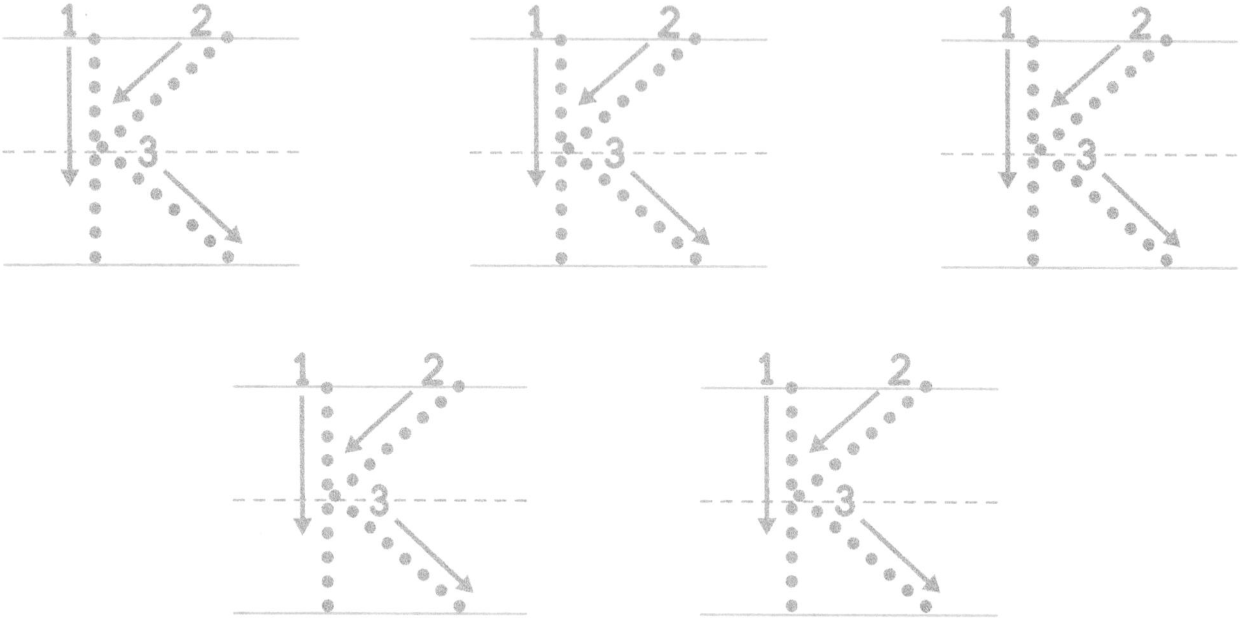

Trace five small letter **k's.**

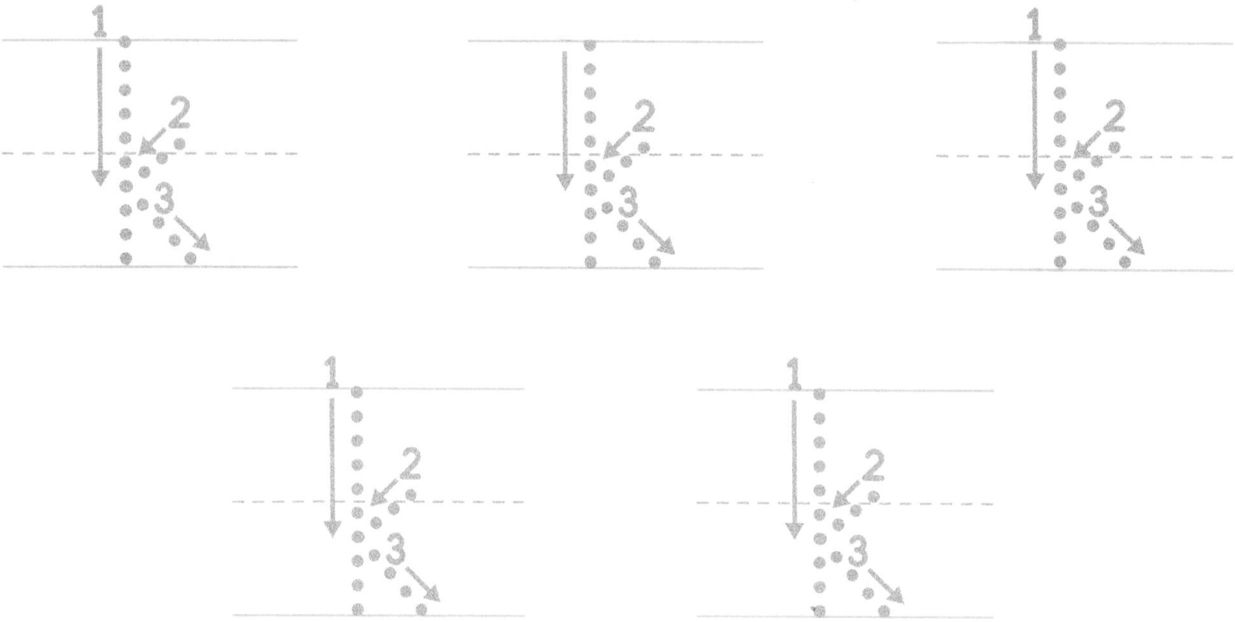

NAME

LESSON 25
WORKSHEET 123

Circle the pictures where the face is sad.

Match the color to the object.

NAME

Tape or paste yarn or ribbon on the picture to show how the men lowered the lame man into the room.

LESSON 26

WORKSHEETS 126-129

Bible Story: Woman at the Well, John 4:1-26

NAME

Letter L

Trace the letters **Ll** with your finger. Color the lion.

Ll

LESSON 26
WORKSHEET 127

NAME

Count the number of leaves in each group and match it to the correct number.

6

7

8

9

10

Trace five big letter **L's.**

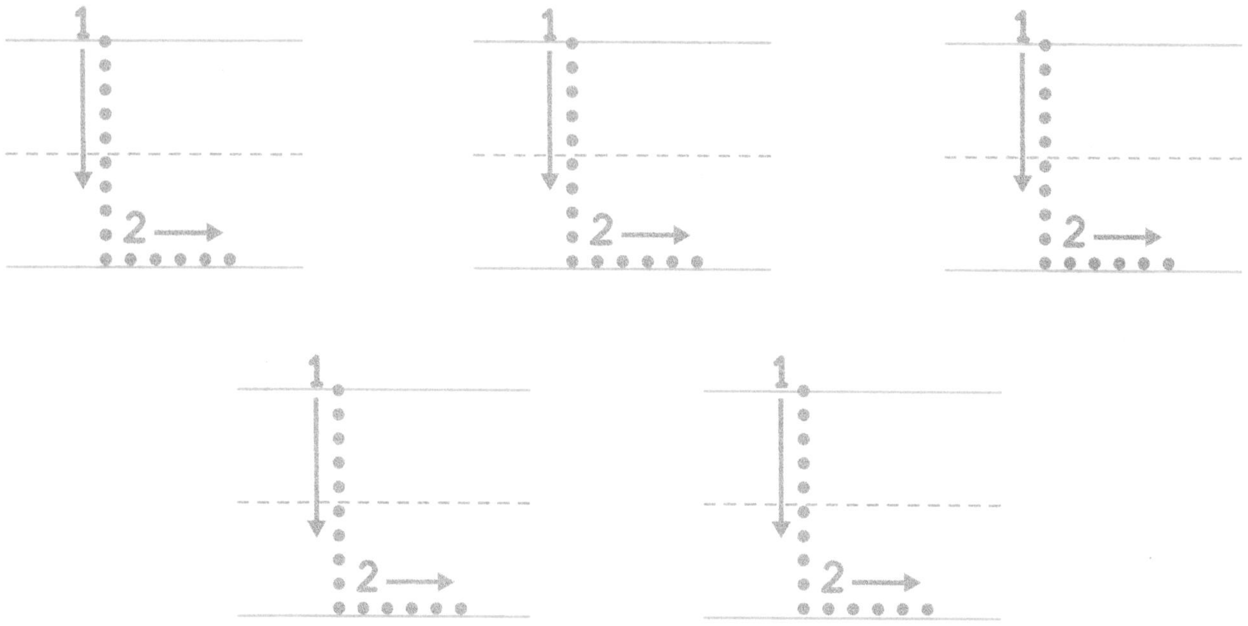

Trace five small letter **l's.**

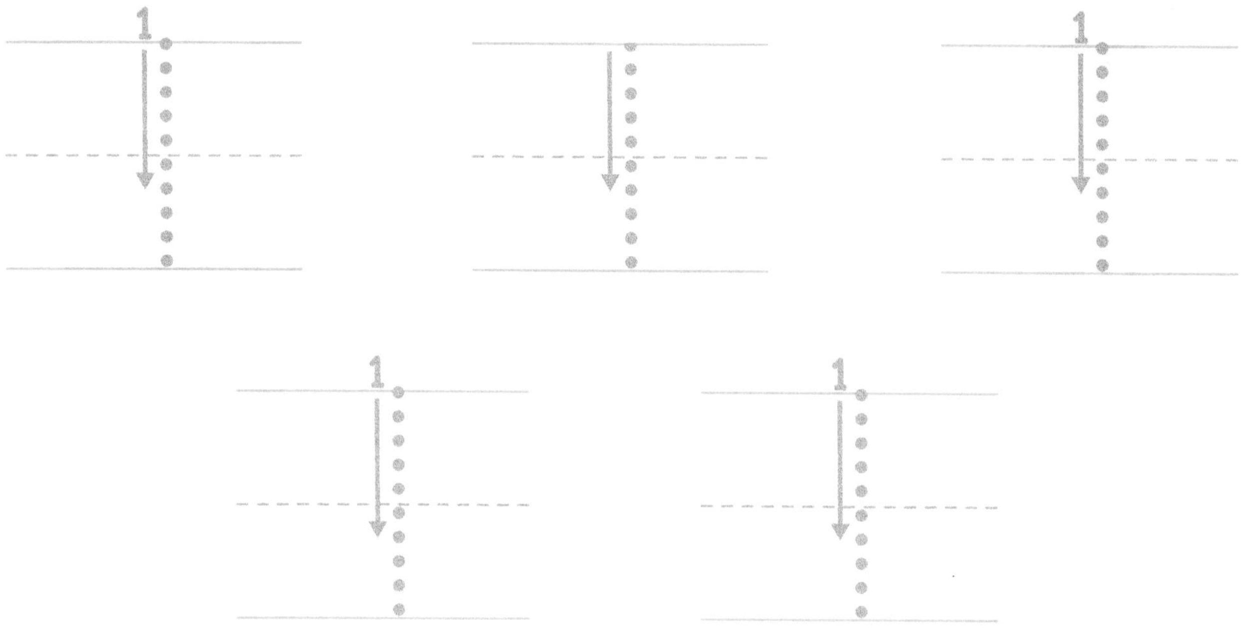

NAME

LESSON 26
WORKSHEET 128

Match the color to the object.

Trace the lines.

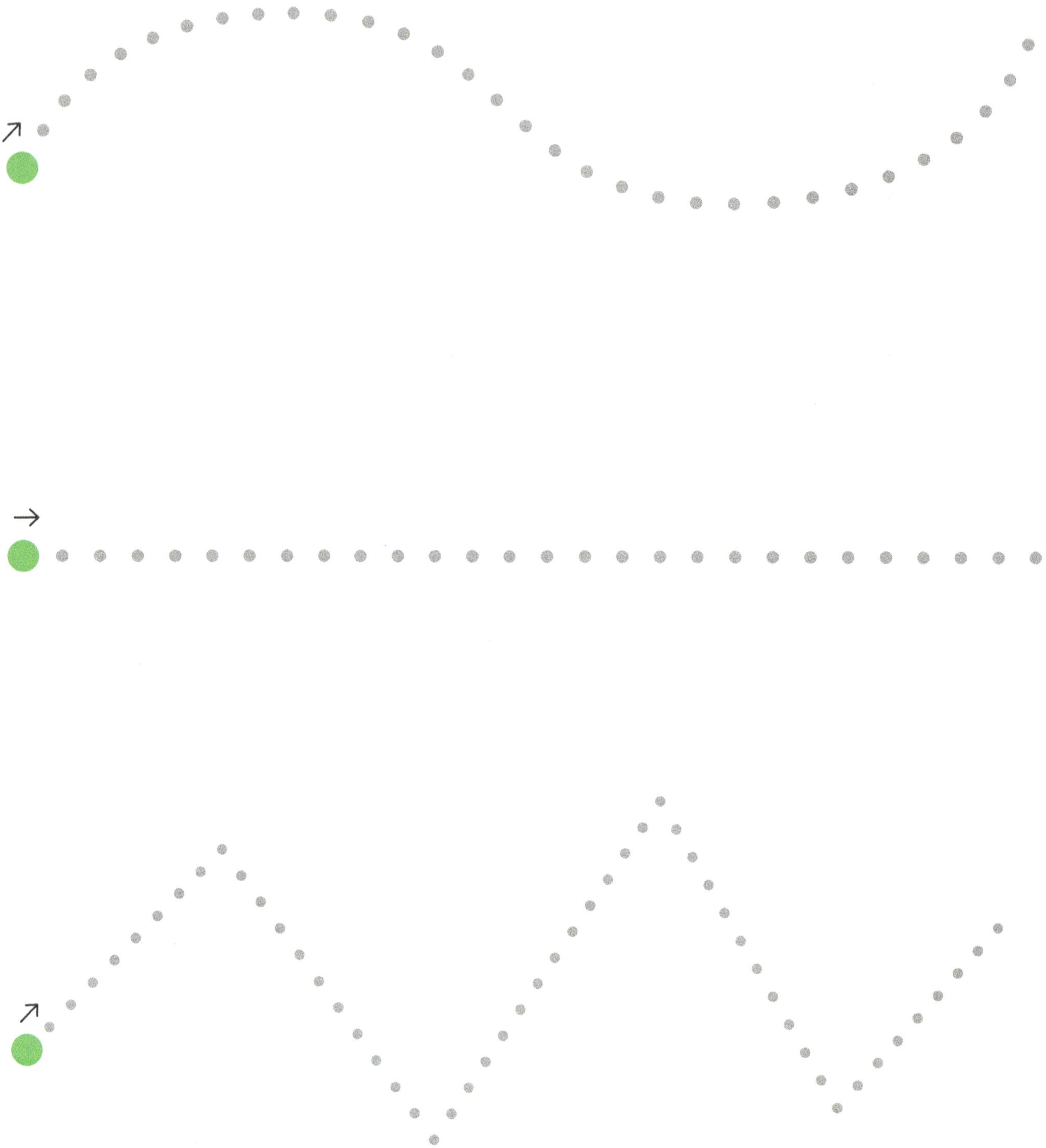

NAME

Color the picture of the woman at the well.

Draw a line matching the numbers that are the same.

1	1
2	3
3	2
4	5
5	4

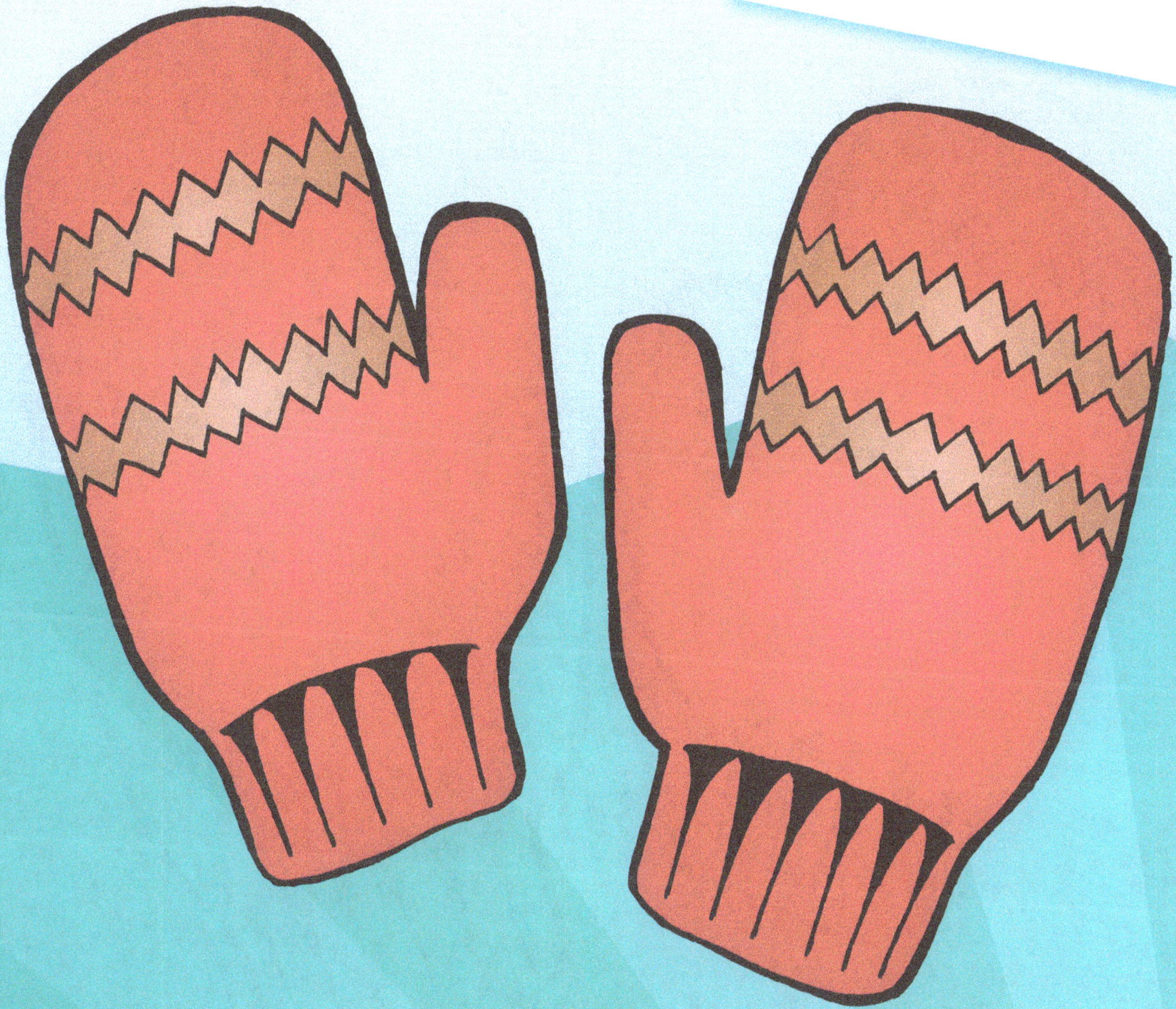

LESSON 27

WORKSHEETS 131-134

Bible Story: Jesus Calms the Storm, Luke 8:22-25

NAME

Letter M

Trace the letters **Mm** with your finger. Color the mittens.

Mm

NAME

Color the picture of spring.

Trace five big letter **M's.**

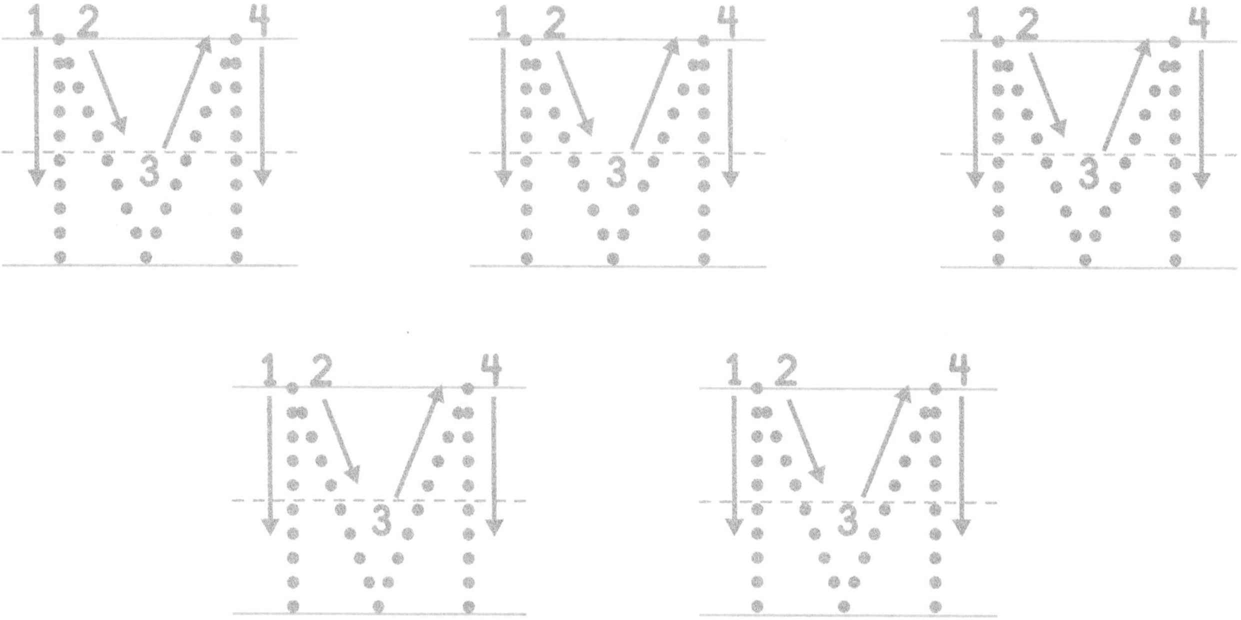

Trace five small letter **m's.**

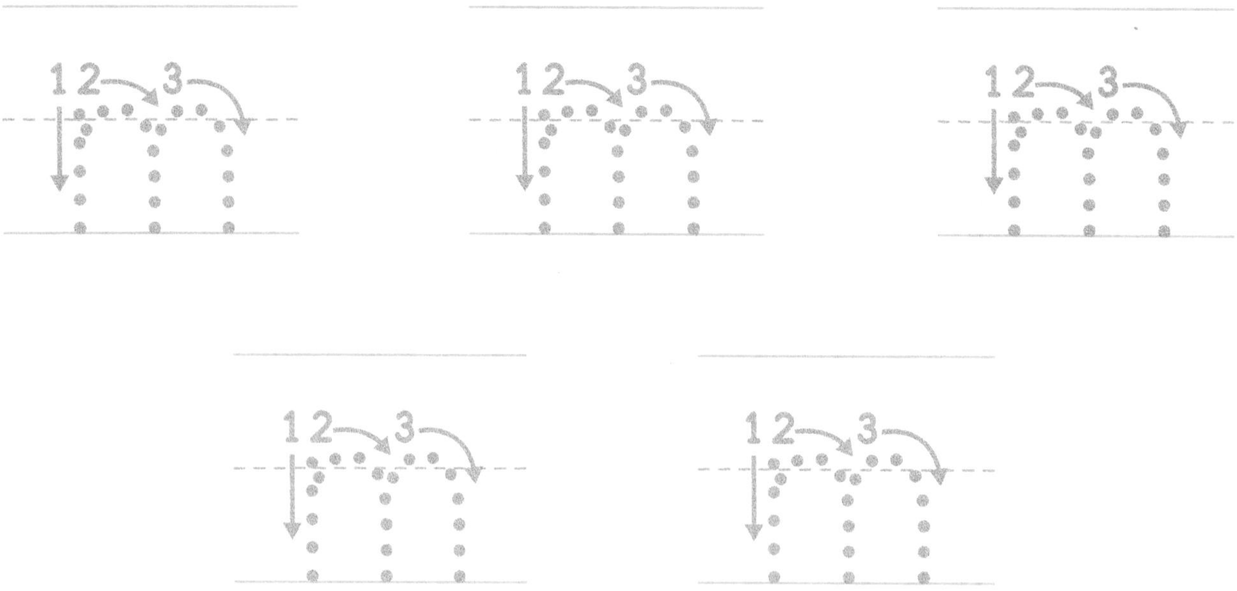

NAME ____________________

LESSON 27
WORKSHEET 133

Circle the items which are hot.
Put an X on the items which are cold.

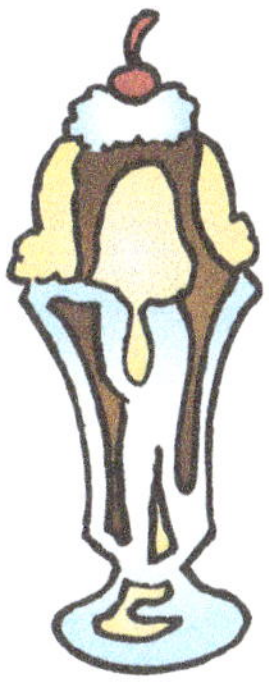

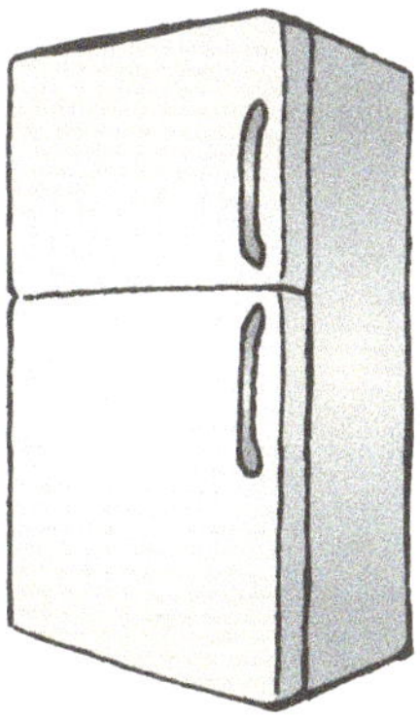

Draw a line matching the numbers that are the same.

6	6
7	8
8	9
9	7
10	10

NAME

Find 5 differences between the two pictures.

LESSON 28

WORKSHEETS 136-139

Bible Story: Raising of Jairus' Daughter, Luke 8:40-56

NAME

Letter N

Trace the letters **Nn** with your finger. Color the nuts.

Nn

NAME

Color the picture of the summer scene.

Trace five big letter **N's.**

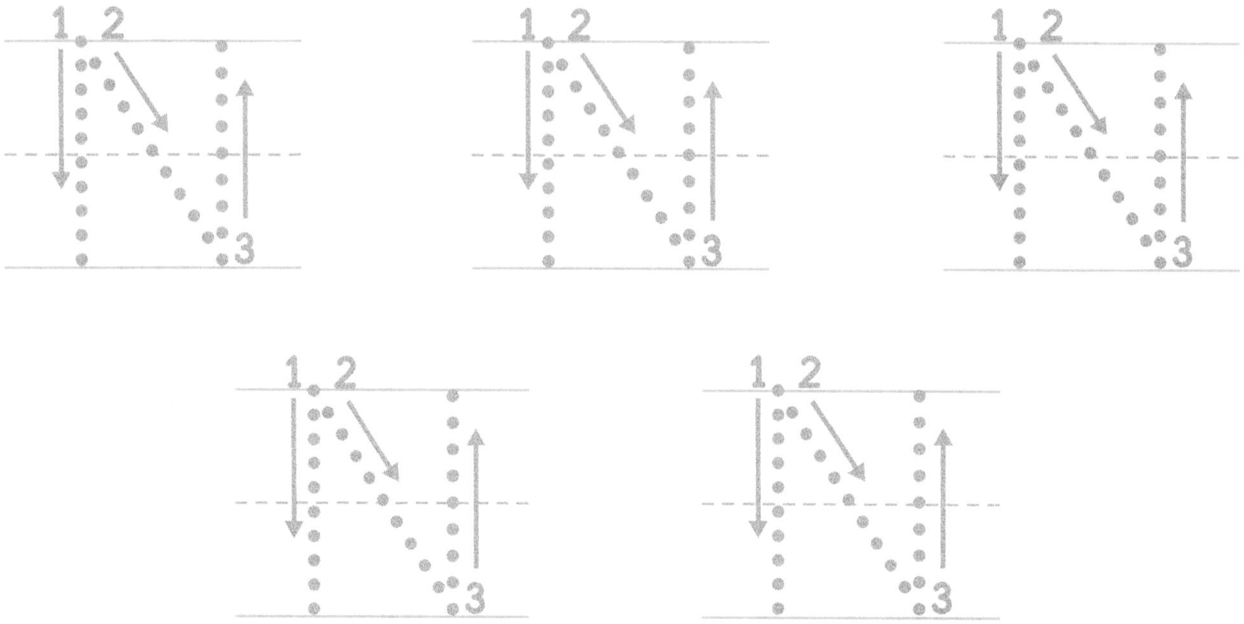

Trace five small letter **n's.**

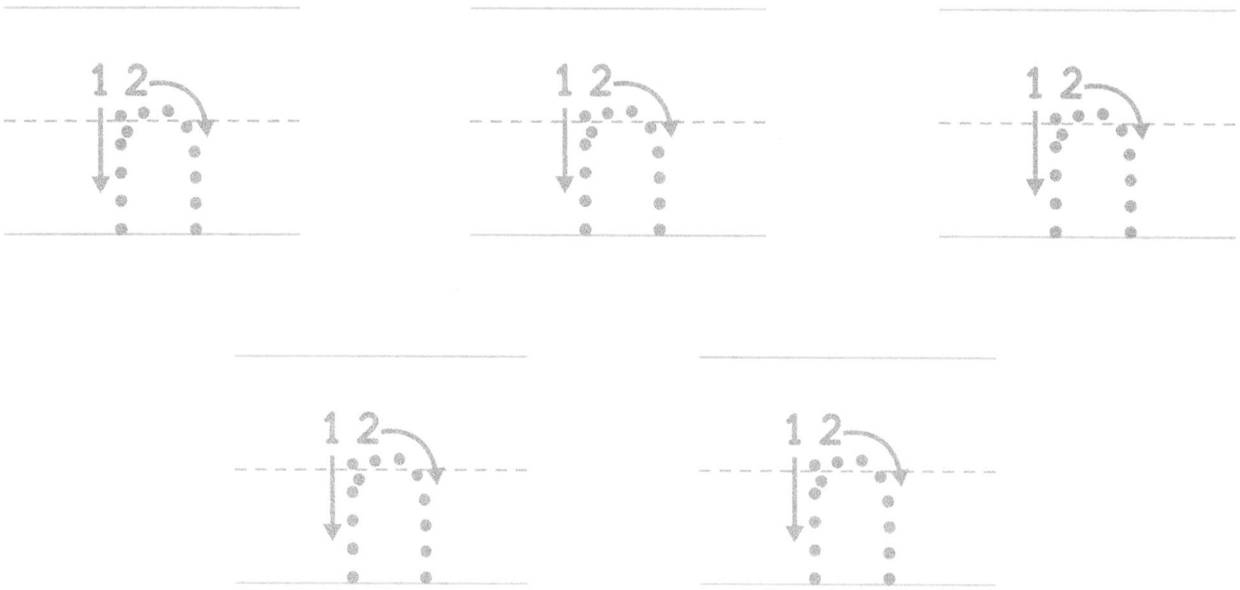

NAME

LESSON 28
WORKSHEET 138

Color the pictures of things you would do in the summer.

Circle the items which are cold.
Put an X on the items which are hot.

NAME

Cut out the puzzle. Put the puzzle pieces together.

LESSON 29

WORKSHEETS 141–144

Bible Story: Jesus Feeds 5,000, John 6:1–14

NAME

Letter O

Trace the letters **Oo** with your finger. Color the ostrich.

Oo

NAME

Color the picture of the fall scene.

Trace five big letter **O's.**

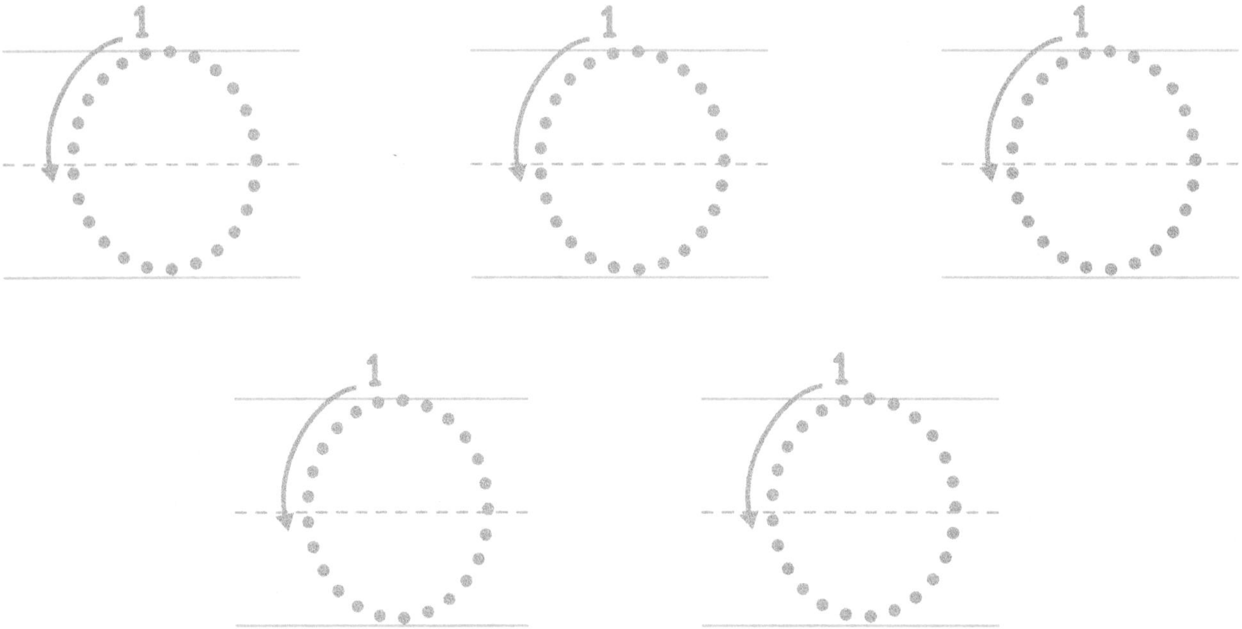

Trace five small letter **o's.**

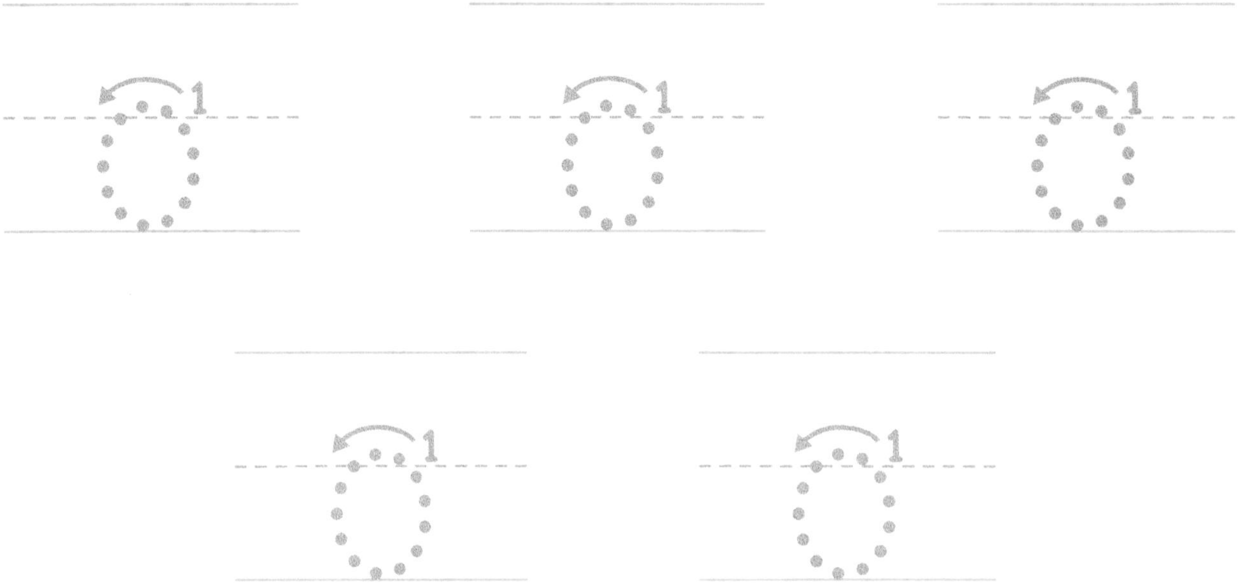

NAME

Put an X on the picture in each row which does not belong.

Draw lines between the items which are opposite.

NAME

Find the five loaves of bread and two fish in the picture.

LESSON 30

WORKSHEETS 146-149

Bible Story: Jesus Walks on the Water, Matthew 14:22-33

LESSON 30
WORKSHEET 146

NAME

Letter P

Trace the letters **Pp** with your finger. Color the penguin.

Pp

NAME

Circle the pictures of things that happen inside the house.

Trace five big letter **P's.**

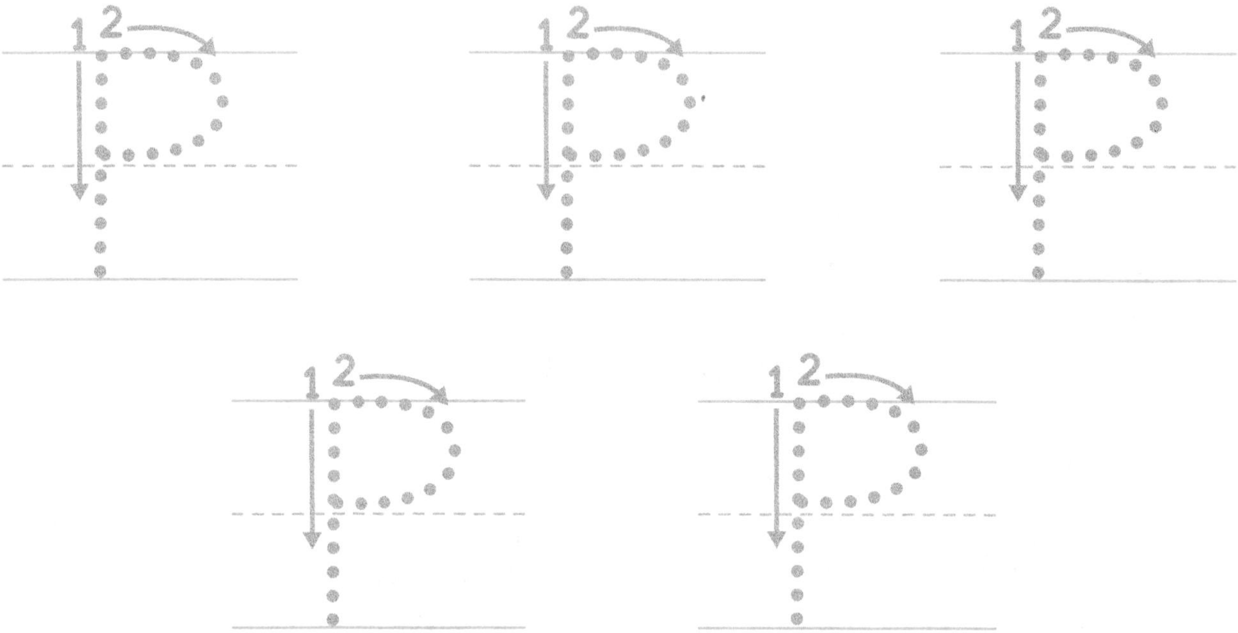

Trace five small letter **p's.**

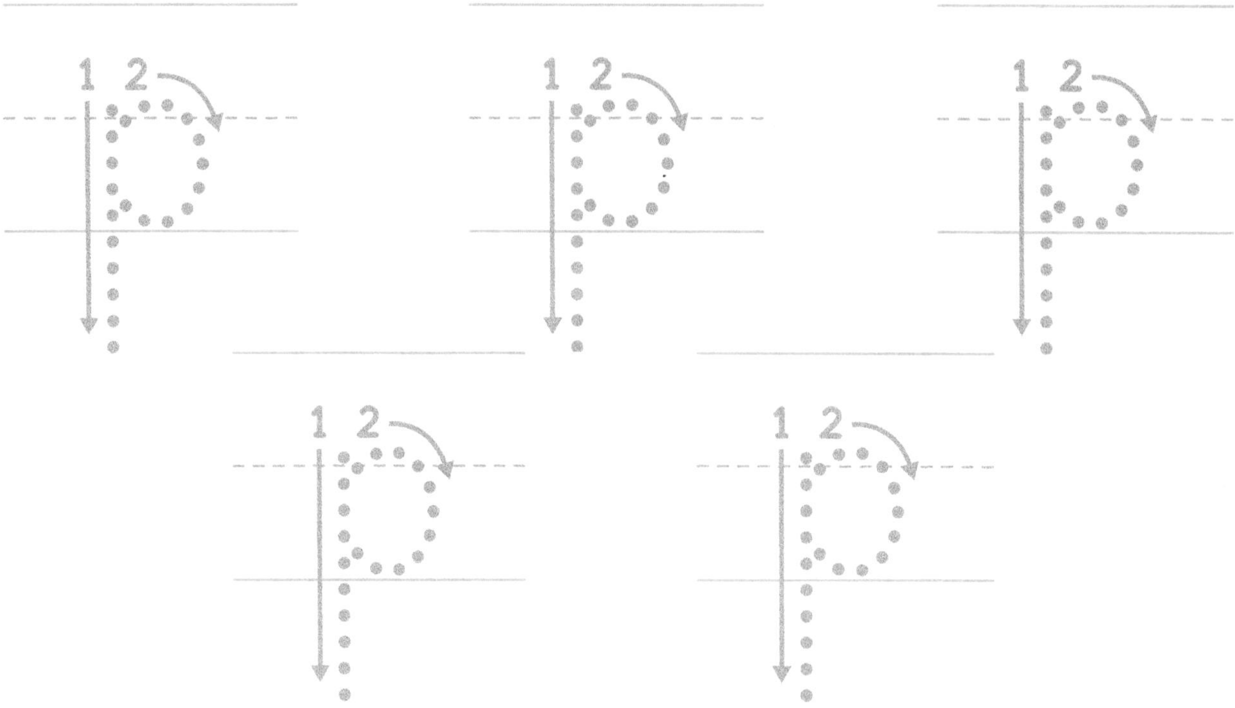

NAME

Circle activities that a person would do in cold winter months.

Draw a line between the item and the part of your body where you would wear it.

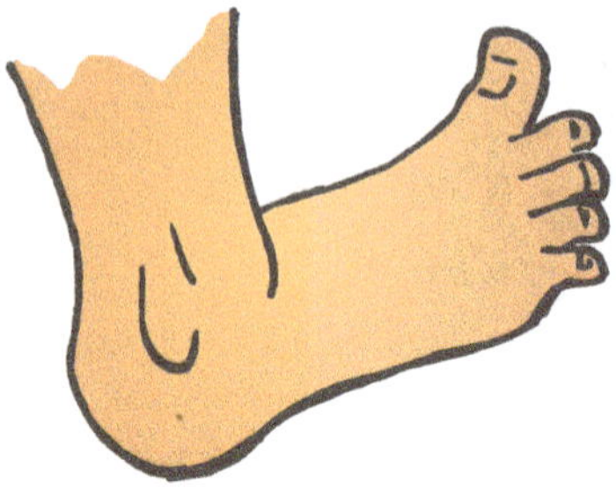

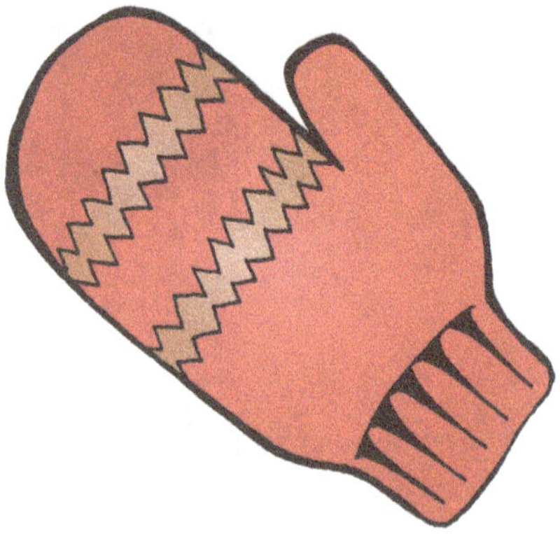

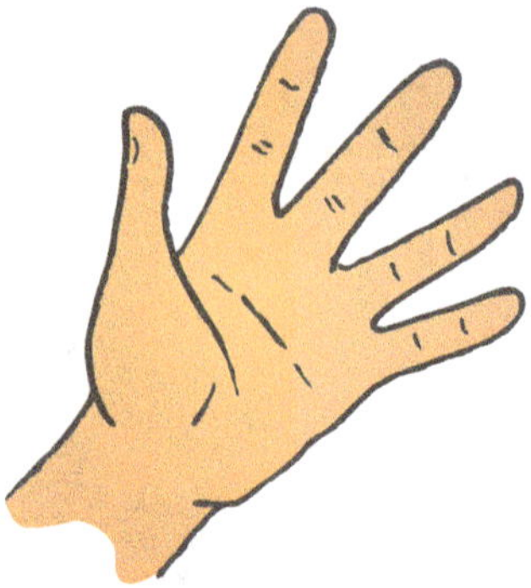

NAME

LESSON 30
WORKSHEET 149

Jesus'  (disciples) were in a  (boat) crossing the Sea of Galilee. The night was dark and  (Jesus) was not with them. When they reached the middle of the lake, it began to storm. The wind blew and the  (waves) were strong. The disciples looked over the water and saw a man approaching. He was not in a . The  were scared. The man was walking on the stormy water.  was the person walking on the water. He called to them, telling them not to be afraid. Once  came near, the  helped Him into the . The  calmed, and they safely reached the shore.

LESSON 31

WORKSHEETS 151-154

Bible Story: Lazarus, John 11:1-44

NAME

Letter Q

Trace the letters **Qq** with your finger. Color the queen.

NAME

Help the queen find her crown.

Trace five big letter **Q's.**

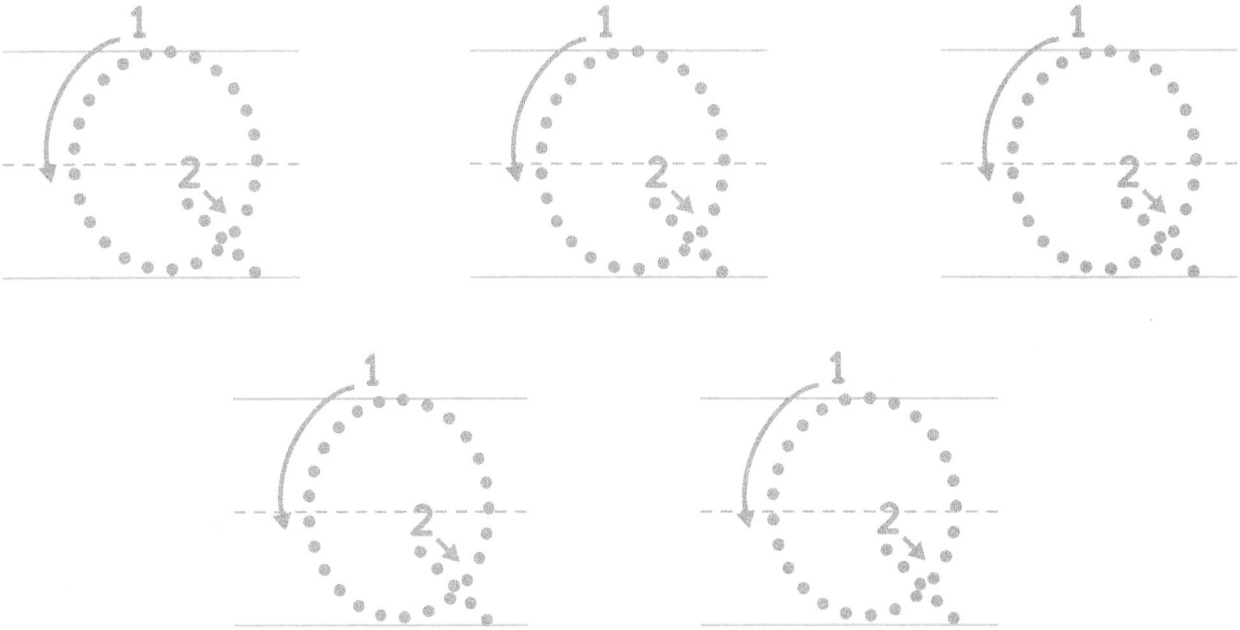

Trace five small letter **q's.**

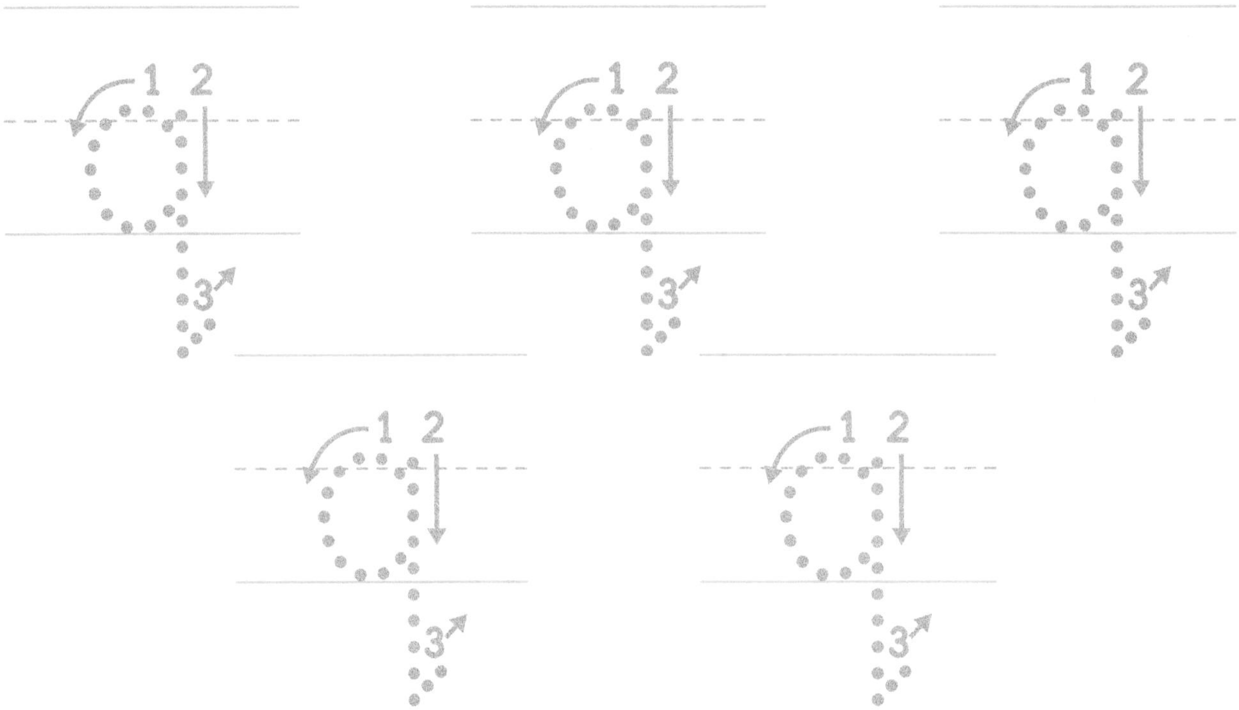

NAME

LESSON 31
WORKSHEET 153

Cut the four pictures apart. Put them in the correct order of spring, summer, fall, and winter.

NAME

Color the words and different shapes on the frame.
Have your parent tape or glue a picture of you in the frame.

LESSON 32

WORKSHEETS 156-159

Bible Story: Jesus and the Lepers, Luke 17:11-19

NAME ______________________________

Letter R

Trace the letters **Rr** with your finger. Color the rabbit.

Rr

NAME

LESSON 32
WORKSHEET 157

Circle the top of each item. Put an X on the bottom of each item.

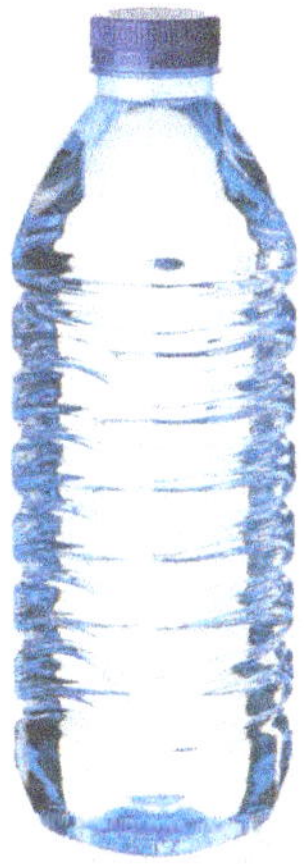

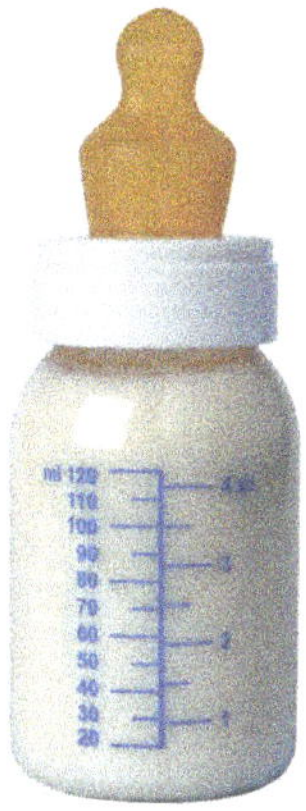

Trace five big letter **R's.**

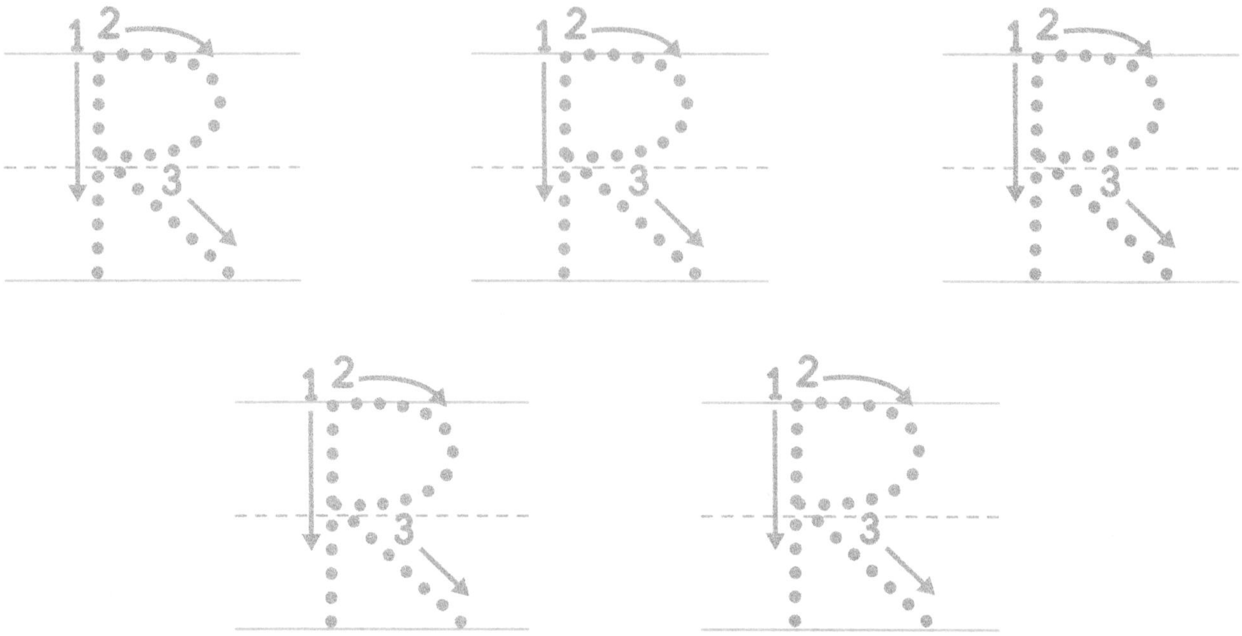

Trace five small letter **r's.**

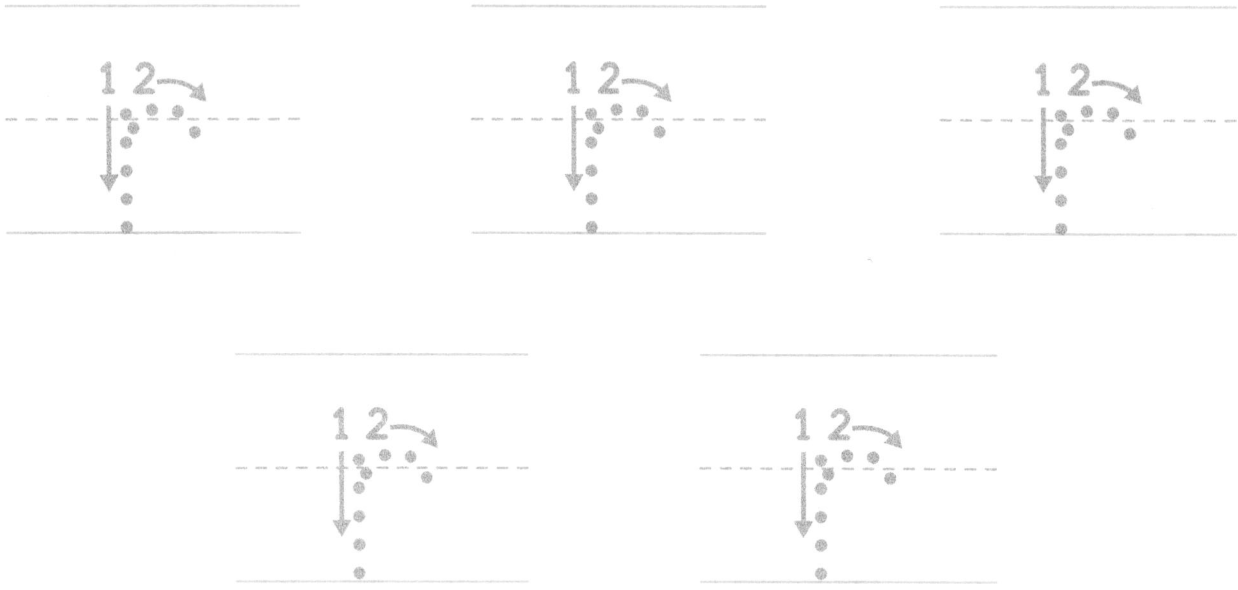

NAME

LESSON 32
WORKSHEET 158

Match items that are about the same size.

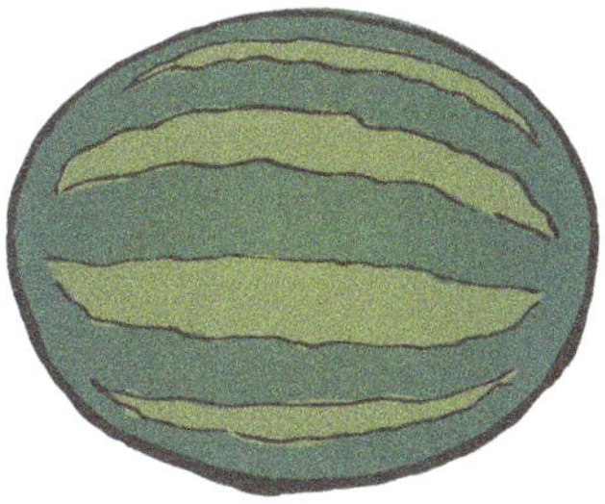

Find items in the house or yard that are the same size as the items pictured on the sheet.

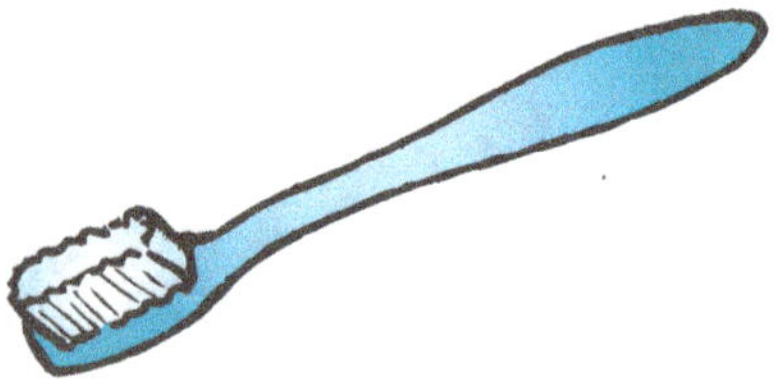

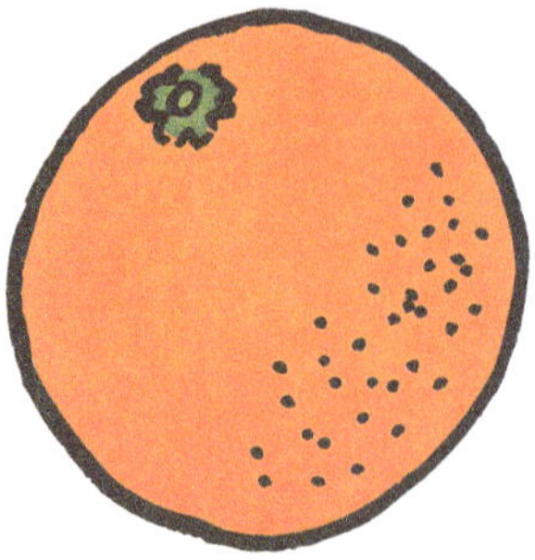

NAME ____________________

Fill in the blanks with things for which you are thankful.

Dear Jesus,

Thank you for the family you gave me,

Thank you that we can ______ together.

Thank you for the food we eat.

Thank you especially for __________.

Thank you for plants and animals.

Thank you especially for __________.

Thank you for loving me.

Amen.

LESSON 33

WORKSHEETS 161–164

Bible Story: Blind Bartimaeus, Luke 18:35–43

LESSON 33
WORKSHEET 161

NAME

Letter S

Trace the letters **Ss** with your finger. Color the socks.

Ss

NAME

LESSON 33
WORKSHEET 162

Circle the doors which are open.
Put an X on the doors that are closed.

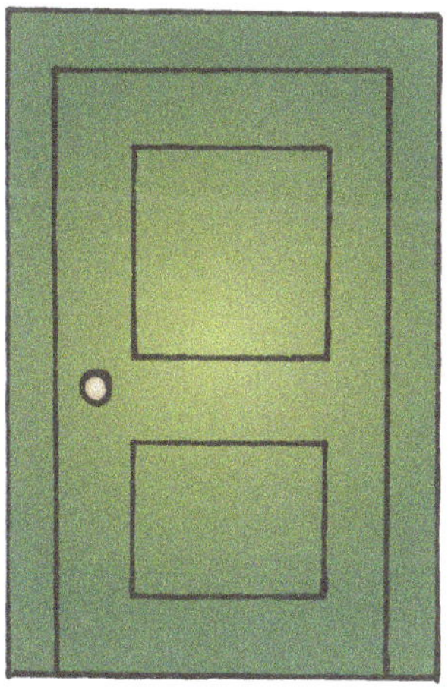

Trace five big letter **S's.**

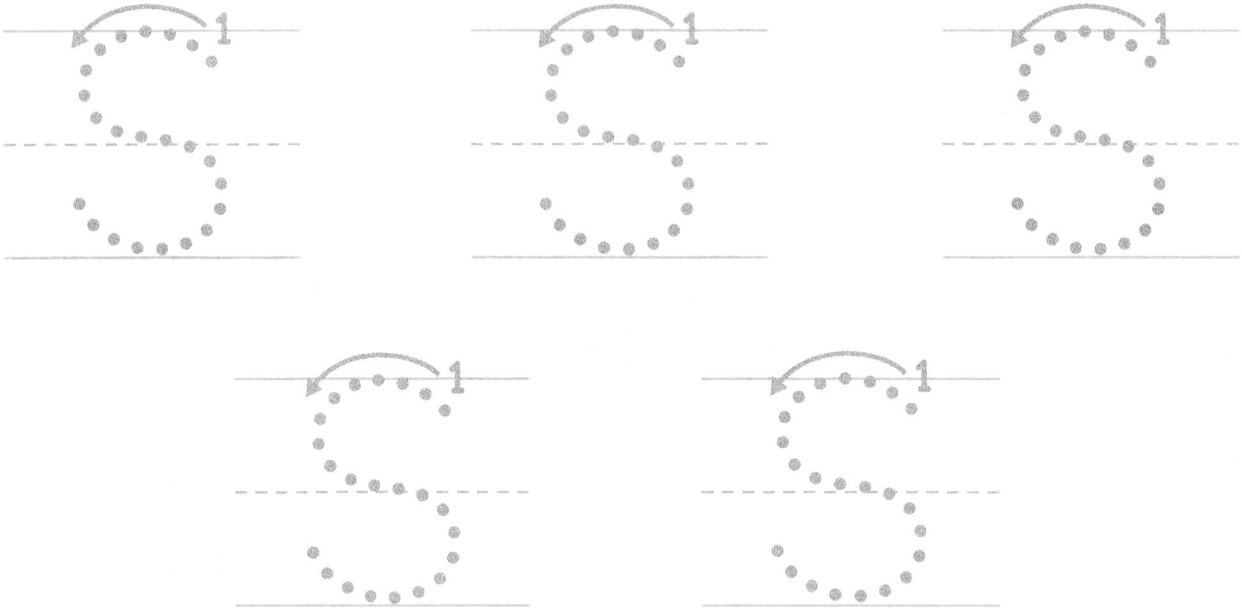

Trace five small letter **s's.**

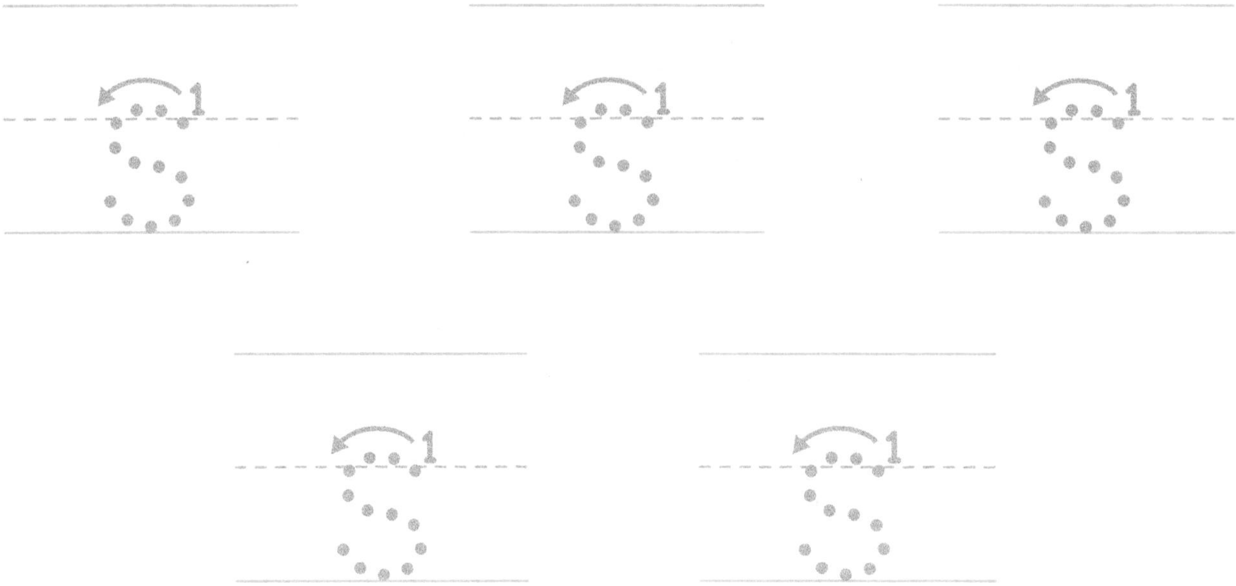

NAME

Circle the item which doesn't belong in each row.

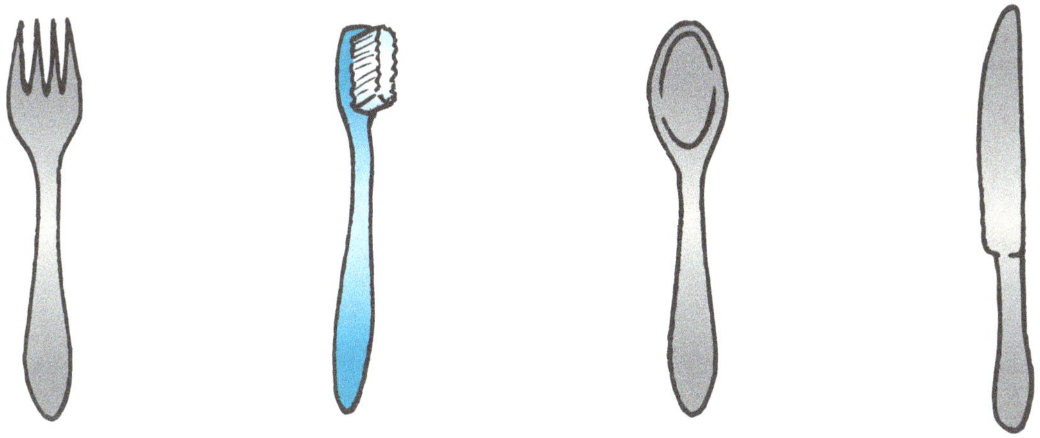

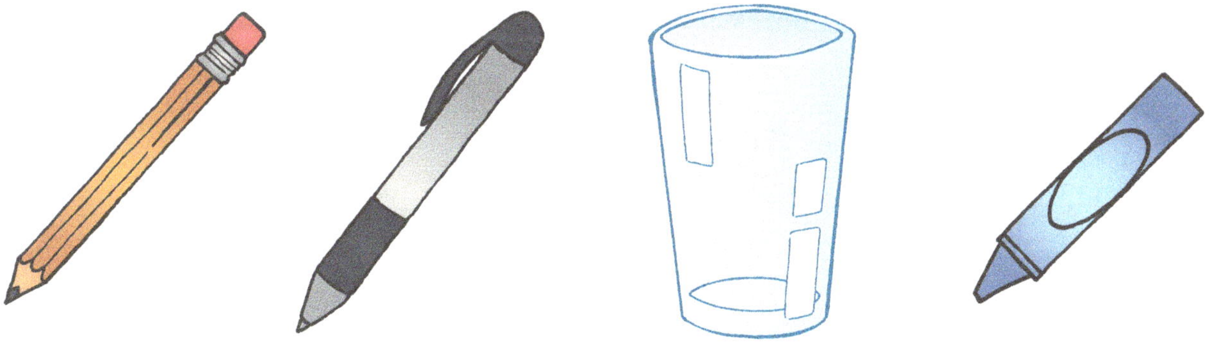

Count the number of socks on each line. Circle the groups of six socks.

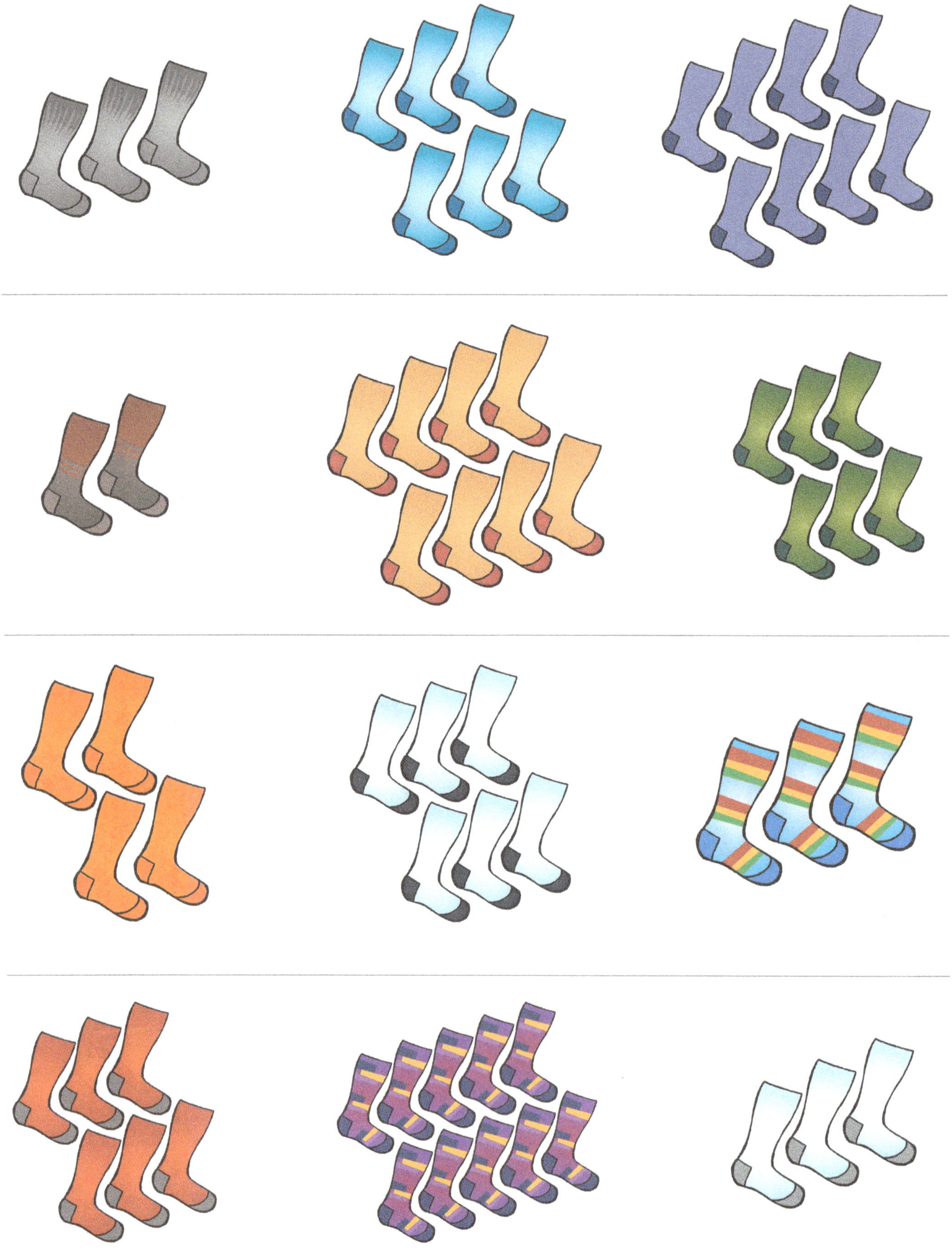

NAME

Find five differences between the two pictures of Bartimaeus.

Circle the pictures of things that happen outside the house.

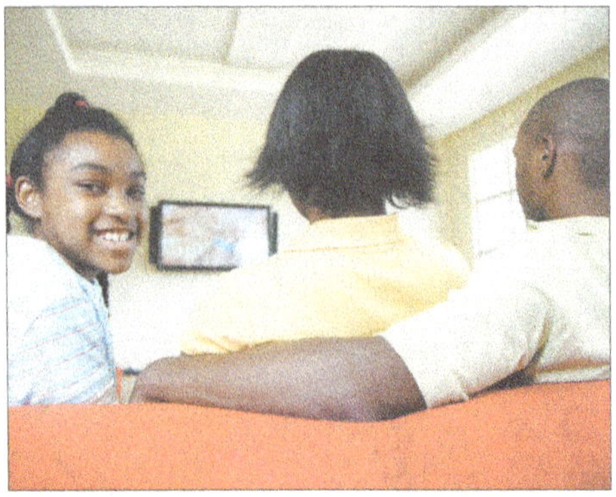

LESSON 34

WORKSHEETS 166–169

Bible Story: Zacchaeus, Luke 19:1–10

NAME

Letter T

Trace the letters **Tt** with your finger. Color the turtle.

T t

NAME

Circle the item in each pair which comes first.
Put an X on the item that comes last.

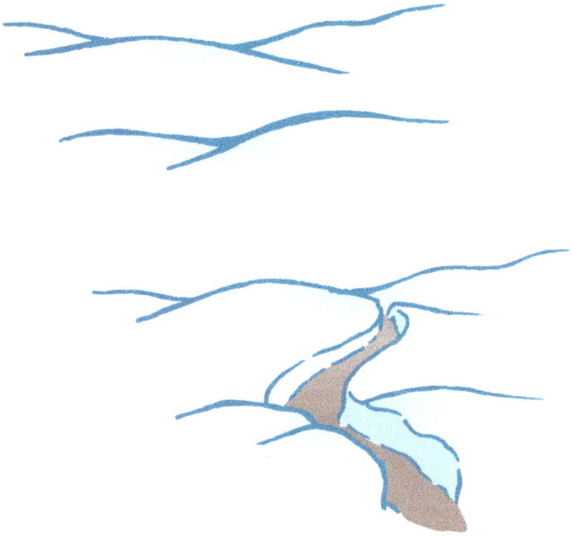

Trace five big letter **T's.**

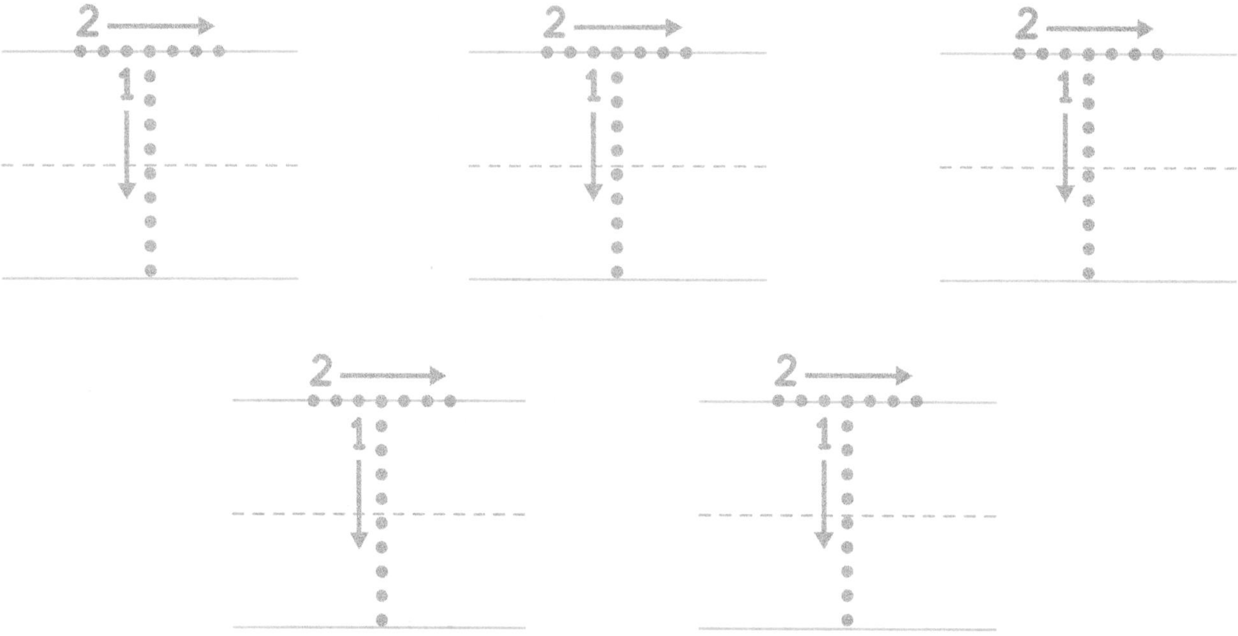

Trace five small letter **t's.**

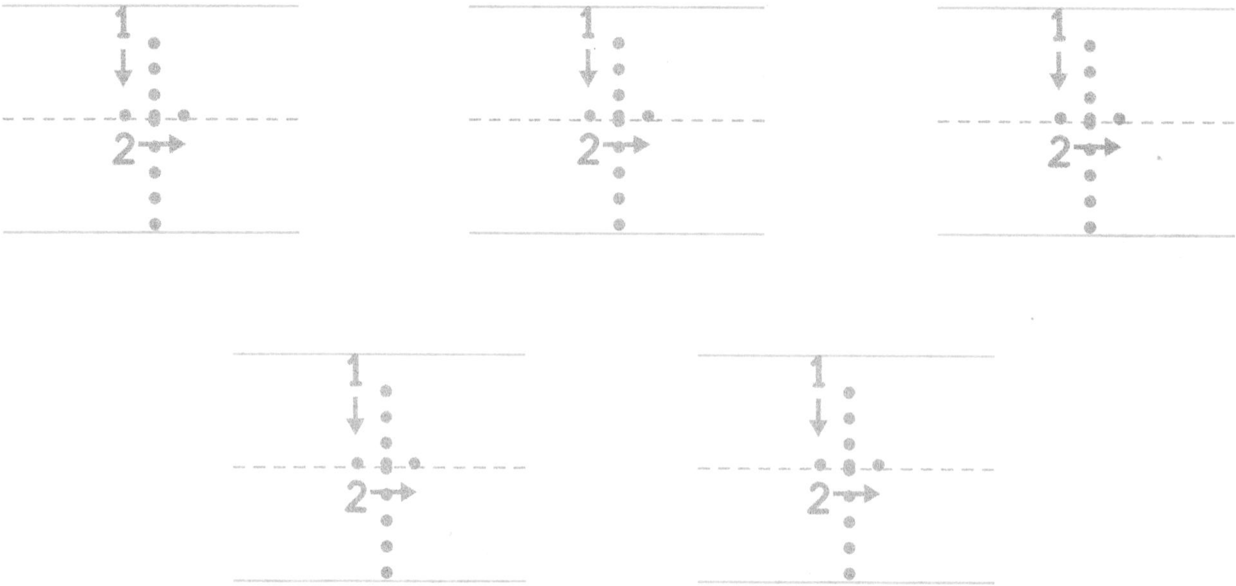

NAME

LESSON 34
WORKSHEET 168

Circle the item in each row which doesn't belong.

Match the item to what can be made from it.

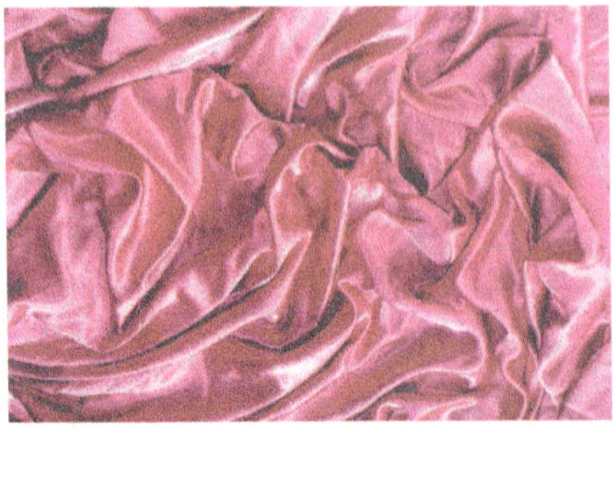

NAME

LESSON 34
WORKSHEET 169

Cut out and use the stand up scene below to retell the story of Jesus and Zacchaeus.

(Tape together the opening on the sides of the ring stands. The larger ring is for the tree and the smaller for Jesus. Fold the tabs on the tree and Jesus at the dashed lines and tape them to the applicable rings.)

LESSON 35

WORKSHEETS 171-174

Bible Story: Triumphal Entry, Luke 19:28-44

NAME

Letter U

Trace the letters **Uu** with your finger. Color the umbrella.

Uu

NAME

Circle what comes first in each group.

Trace five big letter **U's.**

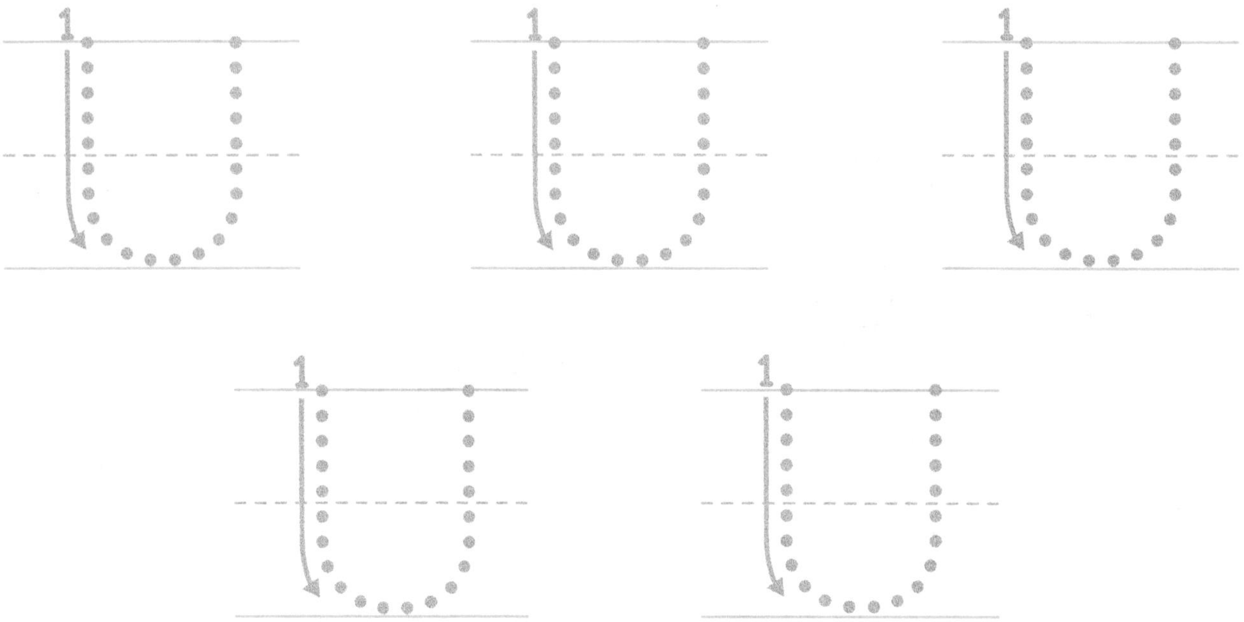

Trace five small letter **u's.**

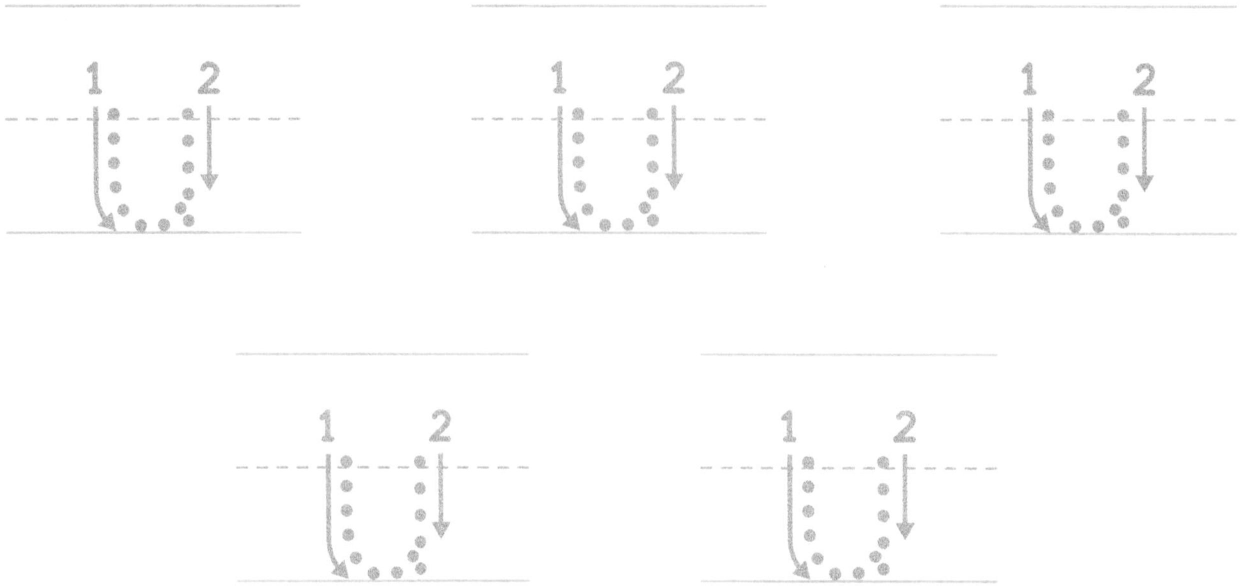

NAME

LESSON 35
WORKSHEET 173

Circle the pictures of good behavior. Put an X on the examples of bad behavior.

Match the activity that takes place in the morning, afternoon, and at night.

Morning

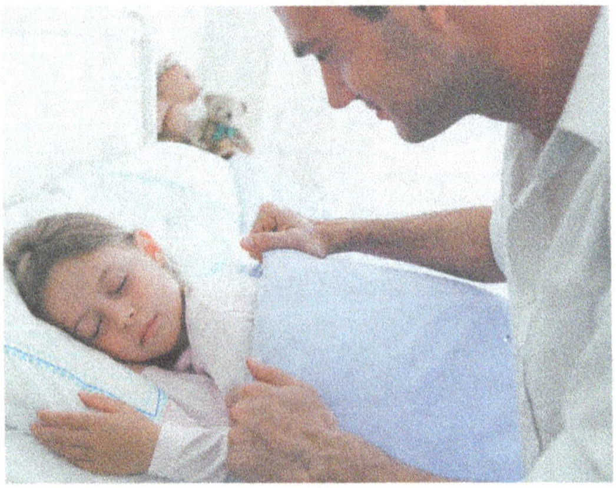

Afternoon

Night

NAME

Cut out the palm branches at the bottom of the page and glue them on the picture.

LESSON 36

WORKSHEETS 176–179

Bible Story: The Last Supper, Luke 22:7–20

NAME

Letter V

Trace the letters **Vv** with your finger. Color the violin.

V v

NAME

LESSON 36
WORKSHEET 177

Tell if the two items are the same or different.

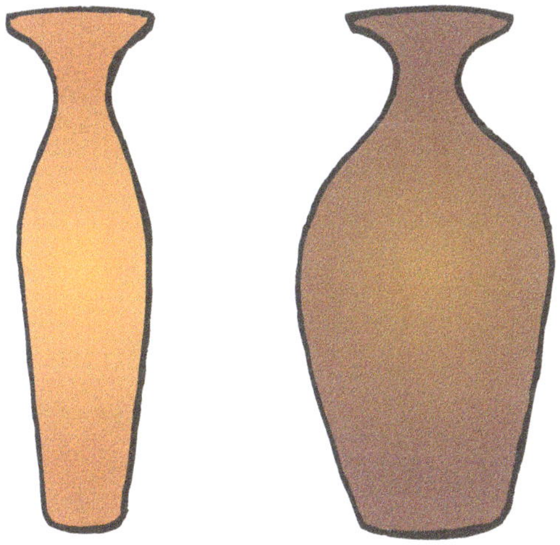

Trace five big letter **V's.**

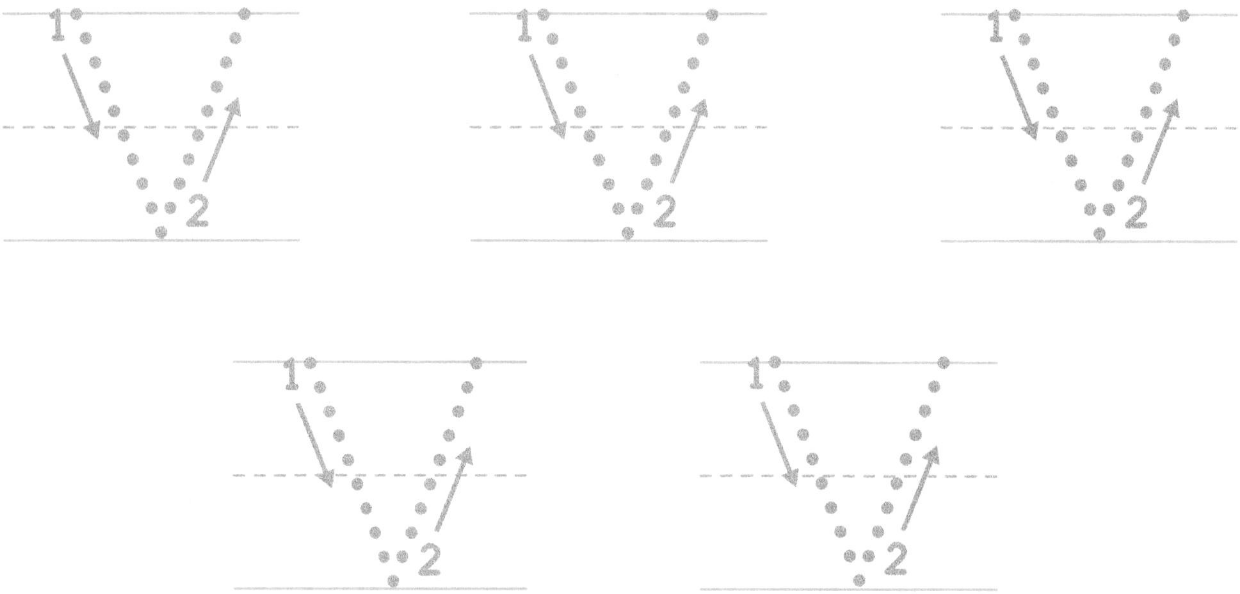

Trace five small letter **v's.**

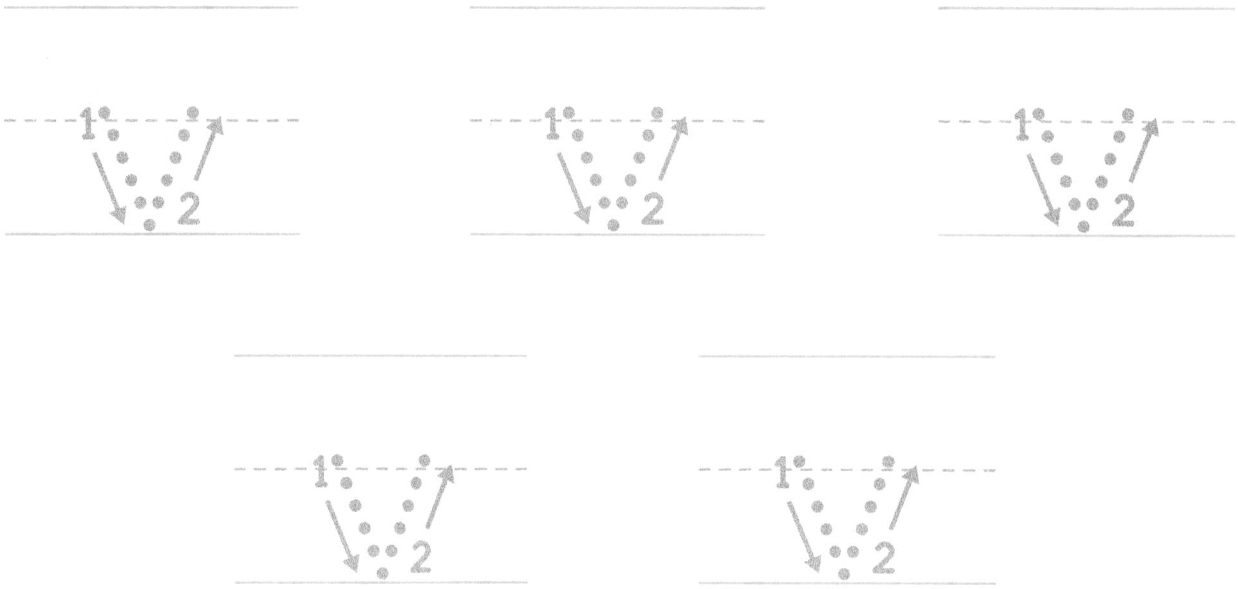

NAME

Cut out the pictures. Put the plants in order as they would grow.

Plant #1

Plant #2

NAME

Connect the dots to complete the bread and the cup. Color the picture.

LESSON 37

WORKSHEETS 181-184

Bible Story: Crucifixion, Luke 22:47-23:56

NAME ______________________________

Letter W

Trace the letters **Ww** with your finger. Color the wolf.

W w

NAME

Color the pictures of different types of weather.

Trace five big letter **W's.**

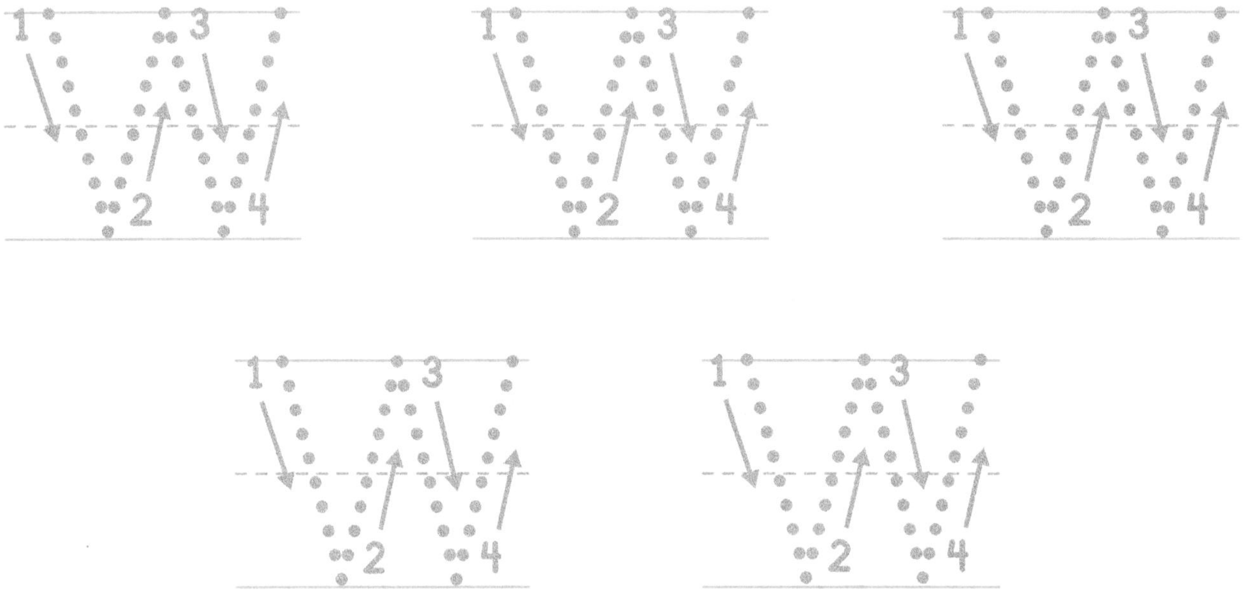

Trace five small letter **w's.**

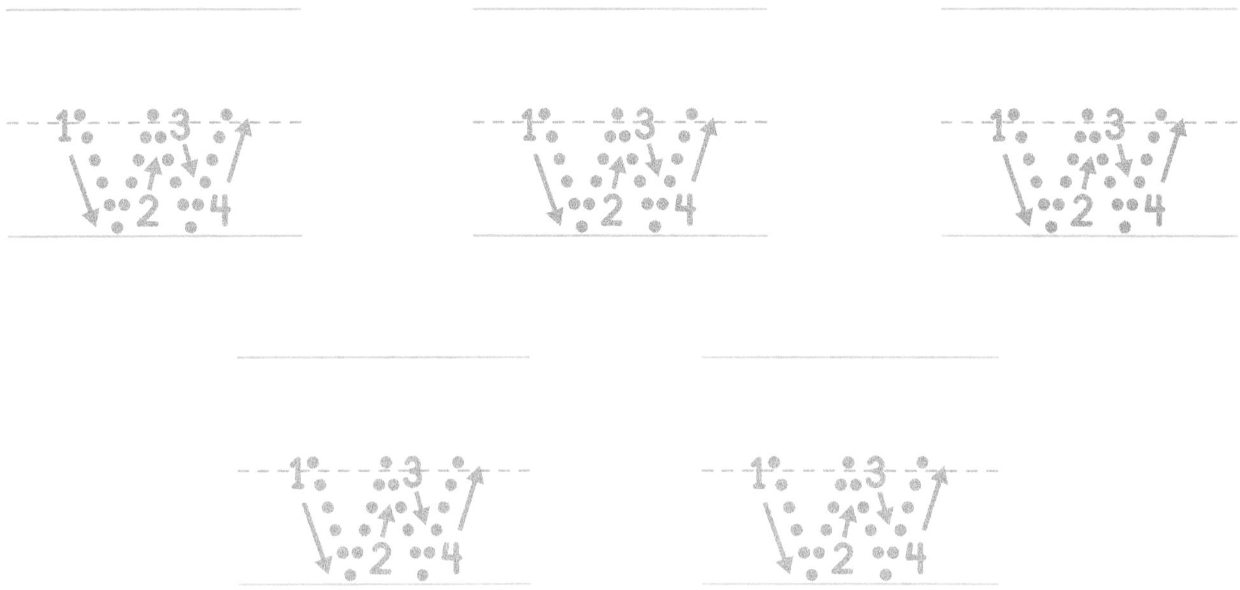

NAME

LESSON 37
WORKSHEET 183

Match the outfit to the type of weather.

Circle the items which are hard.

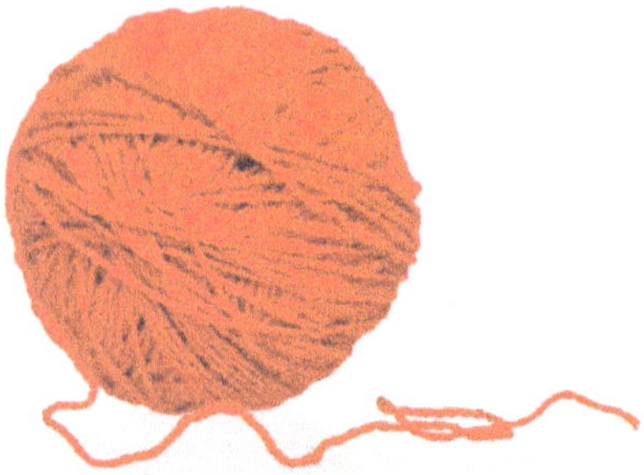

NAME

Color the picture of the Bible story.

LESSON 38

WORKSHEETS 186-189

Bible Story: Jesus' Resurrection, Luke 24:1–12

LESSON 38
WORKSHEET 186

NAME ______________________

Letter X

Trace the letters **Xx** with your finger. Color the xylophone.

Xx

NAME

LESSON 38
WORKSHEET 187

Circle the items which are wet.

Trace five big letter **X's.**

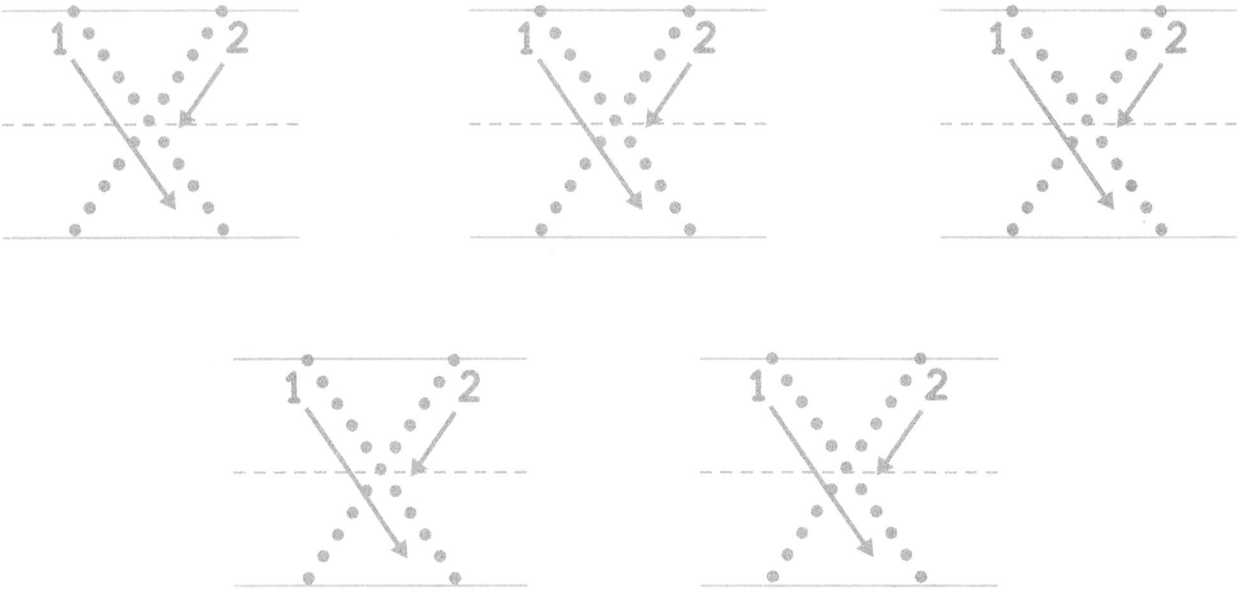

Trace five small letter **x's.**

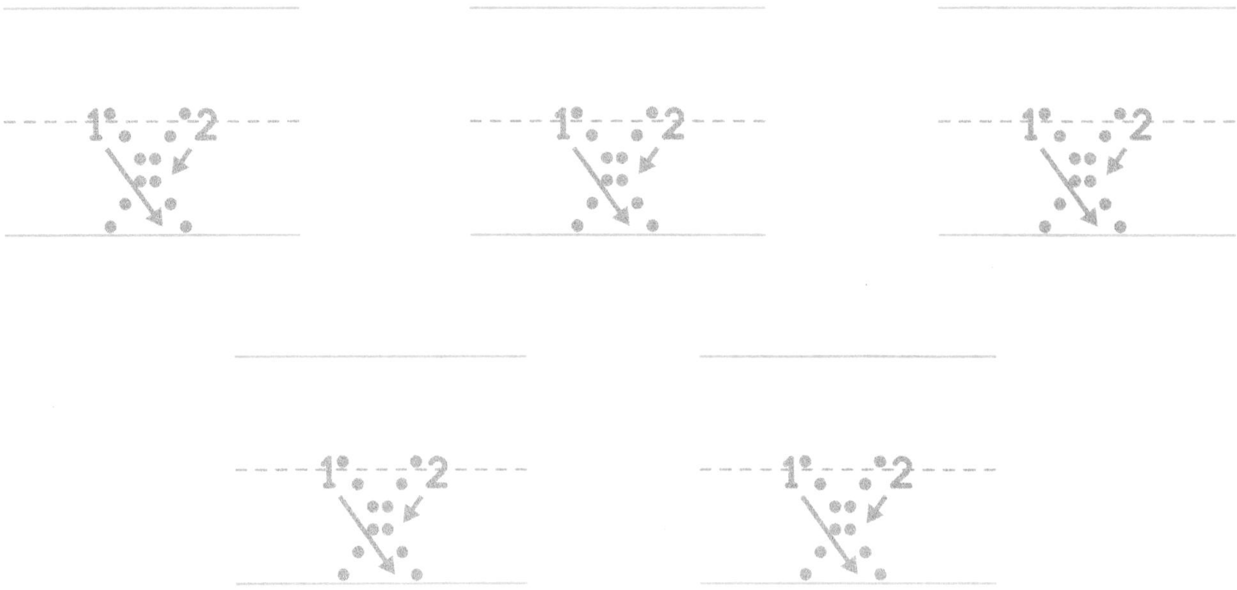

NAME

LESSON 38
WORKSHEET 188

Match the item with the object to which it belongs.

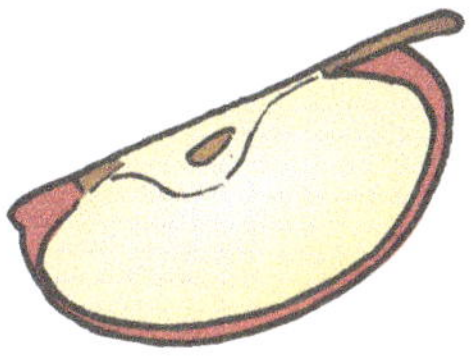

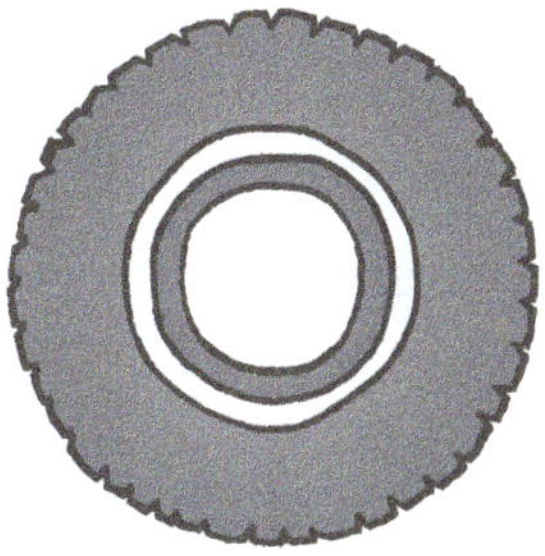

Circle the object which can be used to make the first item in each row.

 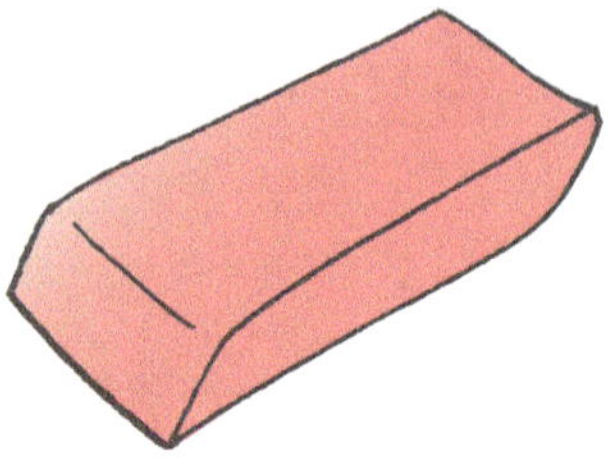 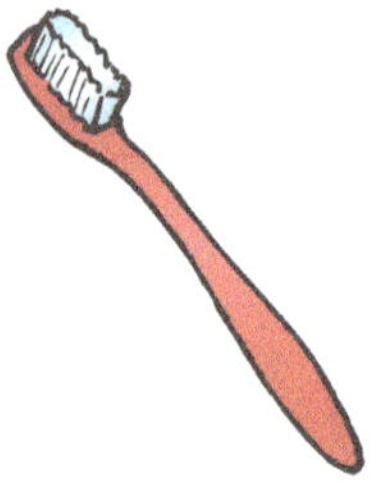 

 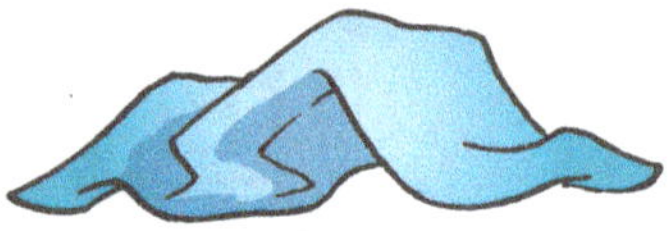  

NAME

Cut out the pictures. Connect the rock to the tomb at the (+) with a brass brad fastener so the tomb can be opened and closed.

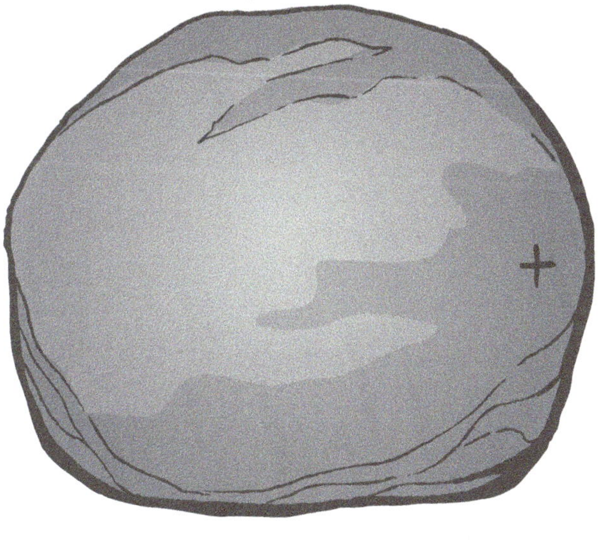

LESSON 39

WORKSHEETS 191–194

Bible Story: Ascension, Acts 1:1–11

NAME

Letter Y

Trace the letters **Yy** with your finger. Color the yarn.

Yy

NAME

Count the number of items in each square.

Trace five big letter **Y's.**

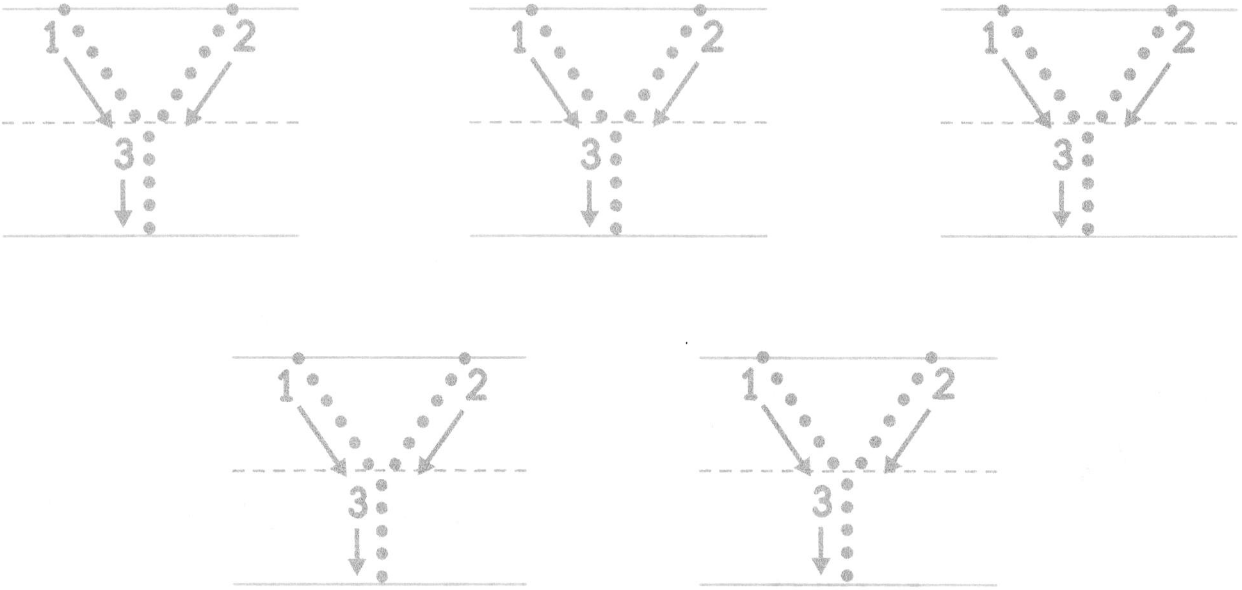

Trace five small letter **y's.**

NAME

LESSON 39
WORKSHEET 193

Match the part of the item to the entire item.

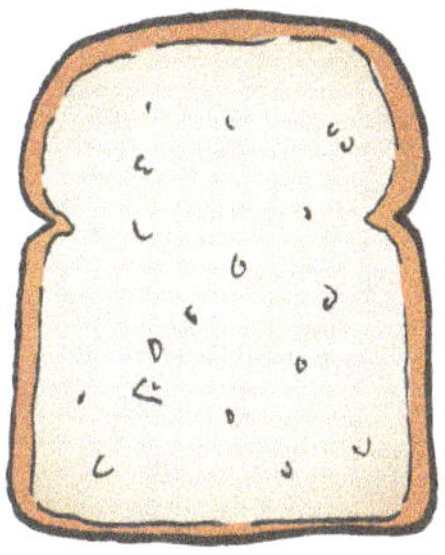

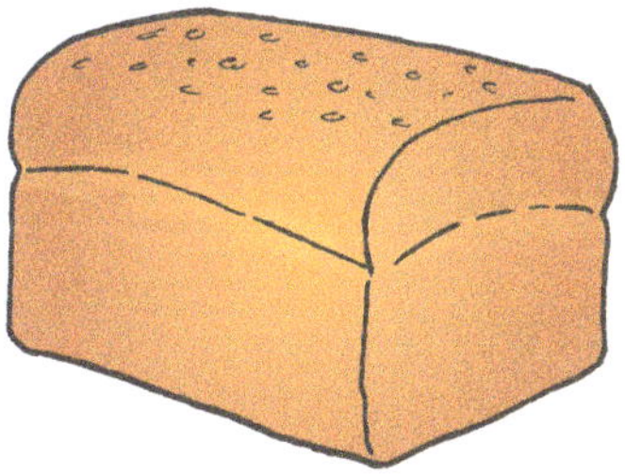

Circle the rough objects.

NAME

Cut out the pictures and use them to retell the story of Jesus' Ascension.

LESSON 40

WORKSHEETS 196–199

Bible Story: The Disciples Preach, Acts 1:12–2:47

NAME

Letter Z

Trace the letters **Zz** with your finger. Color the zebra.

Zz

NAME

LESSON 40
WORKSHEET 197

Match the object to the item it is used to make.

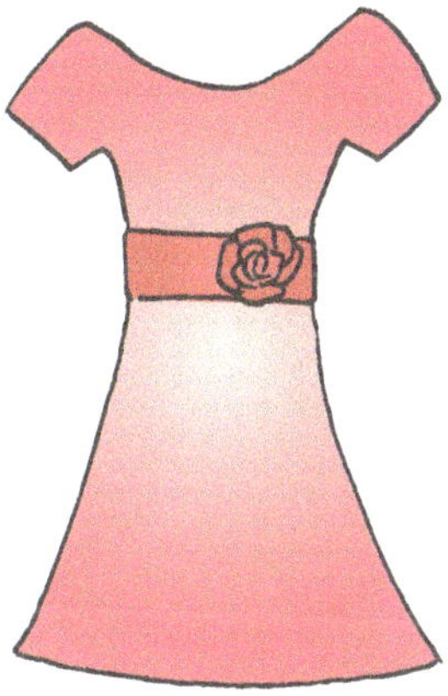
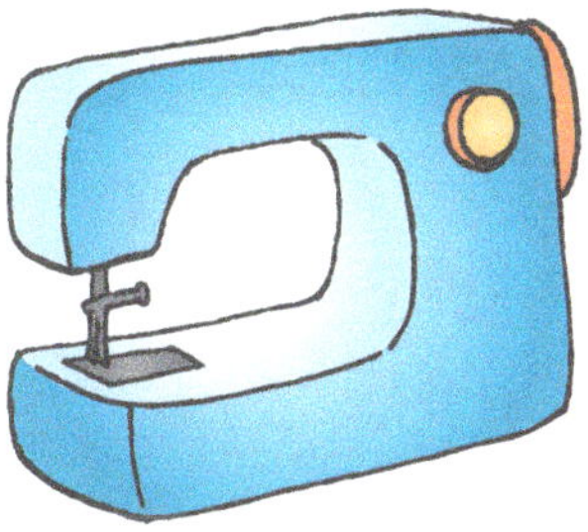

Trace five big letter **Z's.**

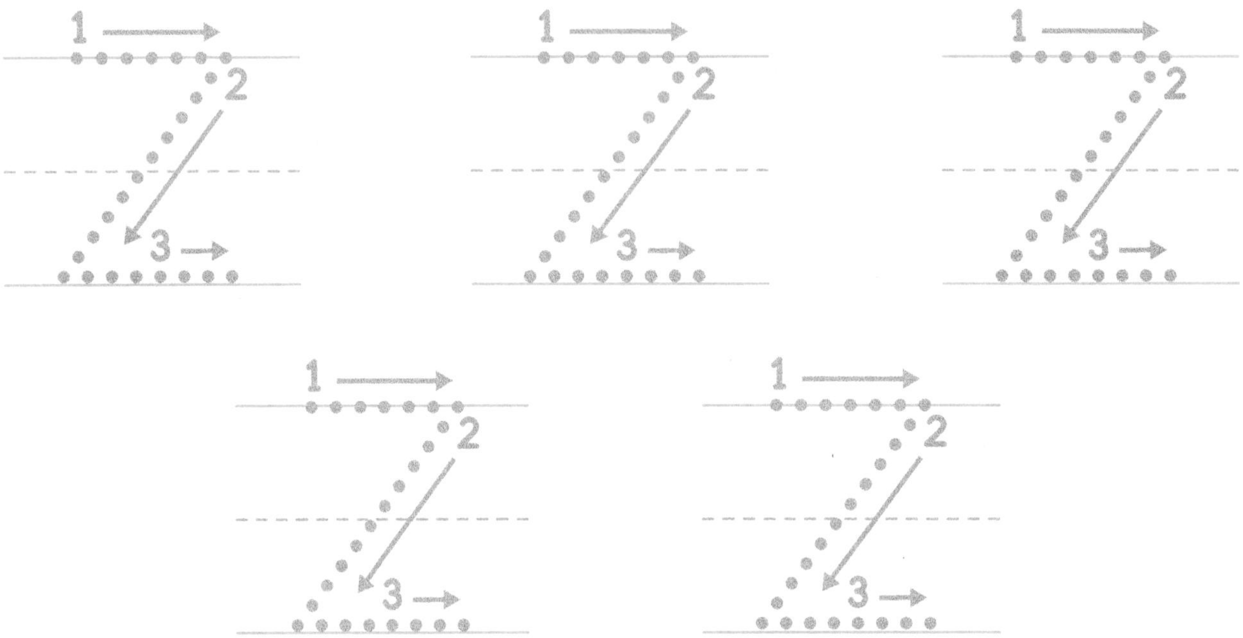

Trace five small letter **z's.**

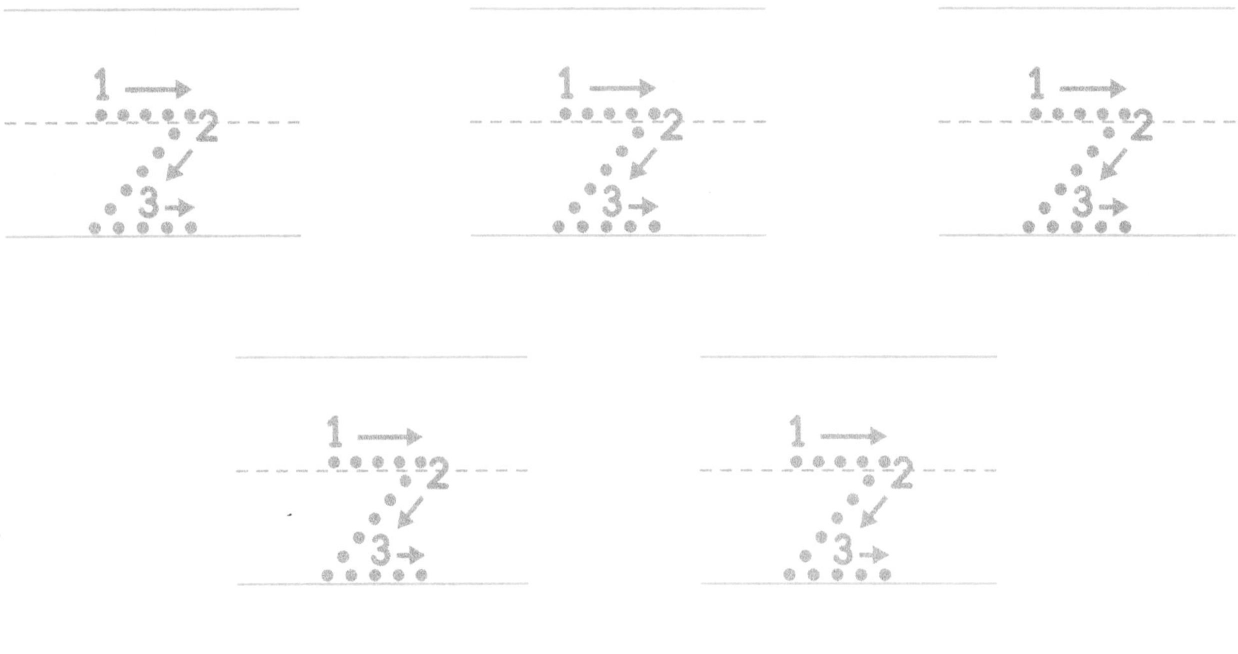

NAME

Choose the item in each row which doesn't belong.

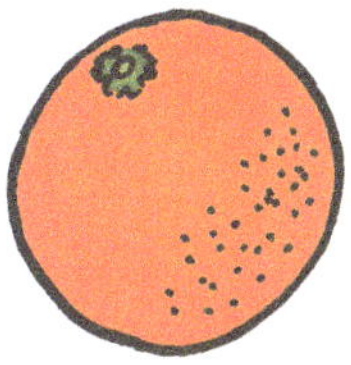

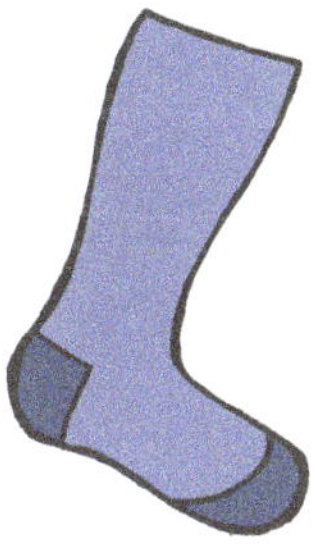

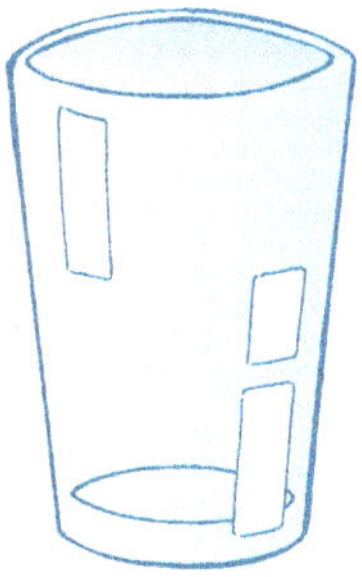

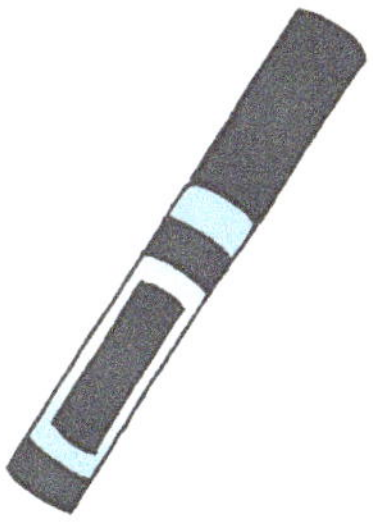

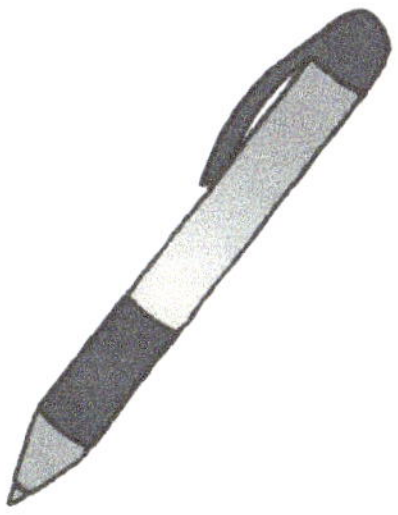

Complete each shape by following the dashes.

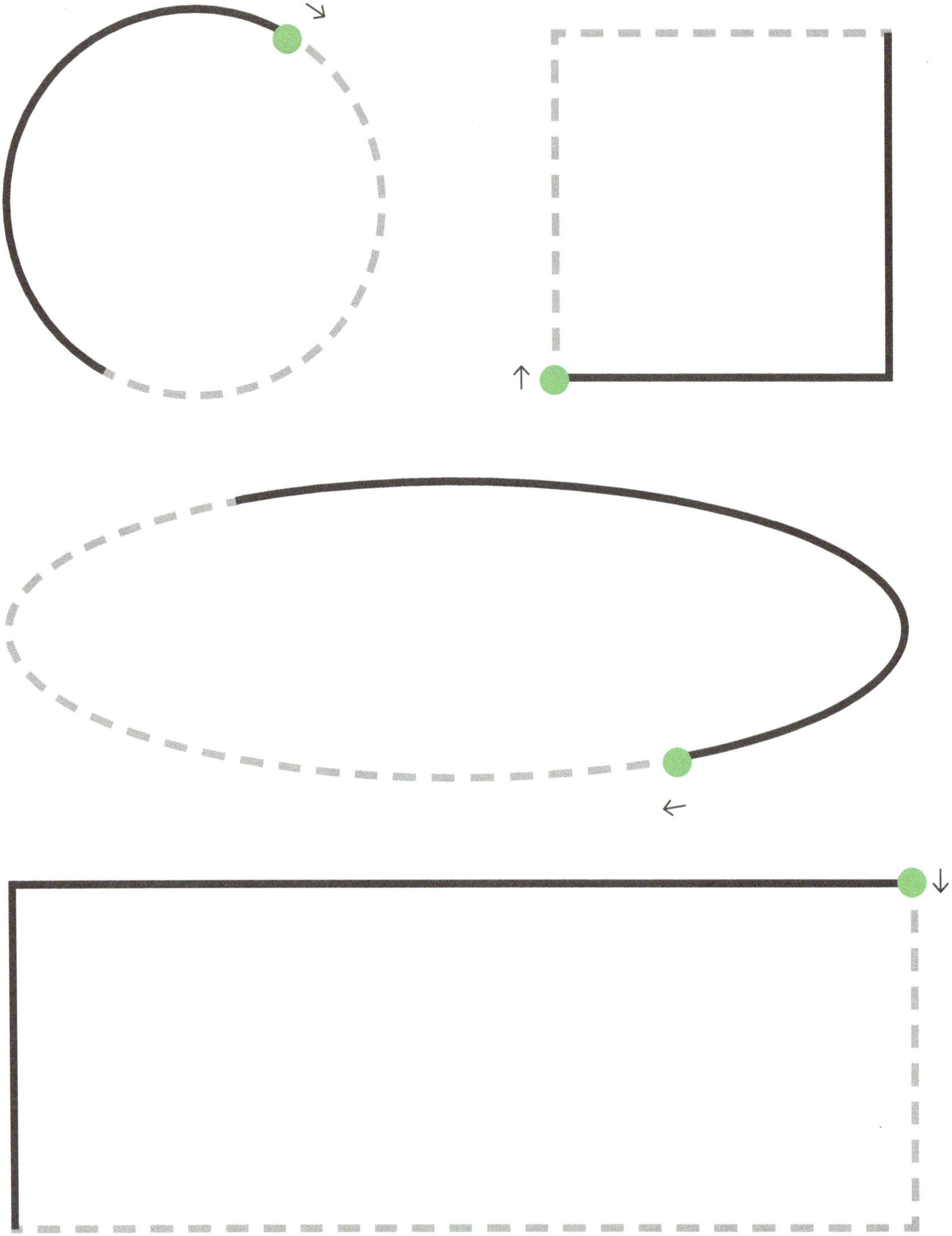

NAME

LESSON 40
WORKSHEET 199

Who can be a disciple?